2020 Vision: The Energy World in the Next Quarter Century

21st Annual Summer Policy Forum
Charles B. Curtis, Chairman

Paul Runci, Rapporteur
John A. Riggs, Program Director

For additional copies of this paper, please contact:

The Aspen Institute
Publications Office
109 Houghton Lab Lane
P.O. Box 222
Queenstown, MD 21658
Phone: (410) 820-5326
Fax: (410) 827-9174
E-mail: publications@aspeninst.org

For all other inquiries, please contact:

The Aspen Institute
Program on Energy, the Environment, and the Economy
Suite 1070
1333 New Hampshire Avenue, NW
Washington, DC 20036
Phone: (202) 736-5823
Fax: (202) 293-0525

Table of Contents

Foreword

Every year since 1977 a group of government and energy industry leaders and others interested in energy policy have convened in Aspen for an Energy Policy Forum on a topic of current and long term interest. These Forums reflect the mission of the Aspen Institute, which is to improve the quality of leadership through dialogue about the values and ideas essential to meeting the challenges facing societies, organizations, and individuals.

The Forums are designed to foster candid exchange among people of diverse viewpoints and backgrounds, and they raise difficult policy questions that require cross-cutting, interdisciplinary debate. Although the participants are experts in their own businesses or disciplines, they are challenged to avoid easy or oversimplified responses that draw on a single area of expertise. The exchanges around the conference table are enhanced by an informal atmosphere and a not-for-attribution rule that nurture creative thinking and candid speaking. Additional opportunities for continued discussion are provided in social and recreational settings surrounding the meeting.

The 1995 and 1996 Forums considered various aspects of the privatization, globalization, and restructuring of the energy industries, largely in a short-term context. In 1997 the Forum took a longer view, taking as its theme *2020 Vision: The Energy World in the Next Quarter Century*. Although acutely aware of the difficulties of predicting the future, the group sought to look beyond the immediate problems associated with restructuring and to consider what the energy world of the future might look like and how it might be influenced by decisions we take or do not take in the next several years. Separate sessions on geopolitics, technology, environment, and market structures focused on these major engines of change, but the richness of the discussion only reinforced the interrelatedness of developments in these areas.

As Chair of this year's Forum we were honored to have Charles B. Curtis, currently a partner of the law firm of Hogan and Hartson, formerly the Chair of the Federal Power Commission and Federal Energy Regulatory Commission, and more recently Undersecretary, Deputy Secretary, and Acting Secretary of the Department of Energy. His extensive experience across a broad range of energy-related issues, his ability to frame the issues in a wide-ranging discussion, and his deft personal touch allowed him to ably conduct this talented orchestra.

In addition to the Chair's valuable leadership, the continuing strength of the Forum rests on the quality of its individual session chairs, its speakers, and its participants. This year's group was outstanding. We are grateful to the session chairs who helped organize an excellent array of speakers and guided the discussions, and to the speakers who brought stimulating intellectual grist for our mill. And because the Forum stresses dialogue rather than didactic presentations as a method of learning, we are especially grateful to the knowledgeable participants, old and new, who challenged, supplemented, and generally helped grind and refine the grist provided by the speakers.

Paul Runci of Battelle, Pacific Northwest National Laboratories served as rapporteur for the Forum, skillfully extracting the major themes and illustrative points from a wealth of excellent presentations and discussions and summarizing them in an interesting and readable text. We are grateful to him and to Battelle, PNNL for supporting his work on this report.

The Aspen Institute and its Program on Energy, the Environment, and the Economy want to acknowledge the very important role of the sponsors of the Program. Without their generosity, support, and confidence in our work, this Forum and the other activities of the Program could not continue.

Thus we gratefully recognize and thank the following for their contributions received during the past year:

ABB Power Plant Systems

The AES Corporation

American Petroleum Institute

Amoco Foundation, Inc.

Arthur Andersen LLP

Bechtel Power Corporation

Cinergy Corp.

CMS Energy Corp.

Destec Energy Inc.

Electric Power Research Institute (EPRI)

Energy Asset Management

ENRON Corp

Equitable Resources

William and Julie Fulkerson

Gas Research Institute

Robert A. Hefner III

Japan National Oil Corporation

Mitchell Energy & Development Corp.

Orange and Rockland Utilities, Inc.

Pacific Gas and Electric Company

Paul Dragoumis Associates, Inc.

PEPCO (Potomac Electric Power Company)

Putnam, Hayes & Bartlett, Inc.

Ruhrgas

Southern California Edison Company

Southern California Gas Company

Verner, Liipfert, Bernhard, McPherson, and Hand

This report is intended as an overview and interpretation of the major themes discussed at the Forum. It is not a consensus document, nor does it attempt to represent all the views presented or represented. Although opinions are occasionally attributed to "some" or "a few" participants, this does not imply that other views reported are unanimously shared. The "Key Findings" quoted in the report are the product of subgroups that reported back to the full group, and thus they can to a greater extent be considered as broadly held views of the Forum. Participants, however, were not individually asked to endorse these findings or their wording.

John A. Riggs
Director
Program on Energy, the Environment,
and the Economy

Forum Agenda

1997 Aspen Energy Policy Forum
**"2020 Vision: The Energy World
in the Next Quarter Century"**

Chairman
Charles B. Curtis
Former Deputy Secretary of Energy
Former Chairman, Federal Energy Regulatory Commission

Session 1:
The Politics of Energy   Sunday, July 6, 8:30 am-12:00

    Chair: **James R. Schlesinger**
               Chairman, The MITRE Corporation

J. Robinson West, Chairman,
    Petroleum Finance Corporation, Ltd.
Alirio Parra, Center for Global Energy Studies
Herman Franssen, President
    International Energy Associates, Inc.

What is the political context in which energy and environmental decisions will be made? How will this affect where we
will be in 2020 and how we will get there? How do the politics
of the environment intermix with the politics of energy? What
are the current domestic and international politics of oil development? Nuclear power? Utility competition and mergers?

1

Session 2: Technology   Monday, July 7, 8:30 am-12:00

Chair: **John H. Gibbons**
        Assistant to the President for Science
        and Technology
James A. (Jae) Edmonds, Battelle - Pacific Northwest
    Laboratories
Trevor Jones, Chairman, Echlin Inc.
Joan Ogden, Center for Energy and Environmental
    Studies, Princeton University
Peter Blair, Executive Director, Sigma Xi, The Scientific
    Research Society

Stipulating that fossil fuels will continue to dominate until 2020 and beyond, what technological advances could allow other fuels to supplement and eventually replace them, e.g. renewables and various options for efficiency gains, including electromotive transportation? What factors will determine whether or not they are adopted?

Session 3: Environment   Monday, July 7, 2:00-5:30 pm

Chair: **Roger W. Sant,** Chairman
        The AES Corporation

William K. Reilly, Founder and Chairman,
    Aqua International Partners
Fred Krupp, Executive Director, Environmental
    Defense Fund

What will be the effects of possible US environmental policies on energy use and energy companies? What factors—scientific, political—will affect the climate change debate? What would be the likely economic effects of a possible Kyoto agreement? What would be the likely environmental effects of no agreement?

Session 4: Market Structures   Tuesday, July 8, 8:30 am-1:00 pm

>   Chair: **Kenneth L. Lay,** Chairman and CEO
>   Enron Corporation
>
>   **Roger Rainbow,** Vice President, Global Business
>   Environment, Shell International
>   **Irwin Stelzer,** Director, Regulatory Policy Studies,
>   American Enterprise Institute
>   **Howard Pifer,** Chairman, Putnam, Hayes & Bartlett, Inc.
>   **Les Silverman,** Director, McKinsey & Company

How will US and world energy markets evolve by 2020? How will demographic trends will affect energy markets? What will energy companies look like? What regulatory structures will be appropriate?

Session 5: Policy Implications   Wednesday, July 9, 8:30 am-12:00

>   Chair: **Charles B. Curtis**

Following the previous sessions, key policy issues arising from the discussions will be identified. In this session, three breakout groups will refine, and perhaps find common ground on, these questions. Then, in a final plenary session, the group will receive reports from the breakout groups and consider a general summation. Moderators of the breakout groups are:

>   **Vicky Baily,** Commissioner, Federal Energy Regulatory
>   Commission
>   **Ben Cooper,** Executive Director, Association of Oil
>   Pipelines
>   **Paul Dragoumis,** President, Paul Dragoumis and
>   Associates

Forum Themes and Conclusions

Introduction

Under the best of circumstances, forecasting is problematic business. In times of rapid and widespread change, efforts to plot the future become even more challenging, as well as potentially more valuable. With this in mind, participants in the 1997 Aspen Energy Policy Forum convened to discuss the dramatic currents of change that are reshaping the energy industries, and to attempt to envision likely and possible energy paths, for the U.S. and the world, over the next twenty-five years.

The geopolitics of energy, which are now evolving and changing in many fundamental ways, provided a broad framework for the Forum discussions. Political and economic reforms unfolding around the world, such as the ongoing processes of democratization in regions such as the Former Soviet Union and the more universal process of globalization, are rapidly transforming the global context in which energy industries perform. In addition to addressing some important dynamics of geopolitical change in and of itself, the Forum focused its attention on three major themes that individually and collectively underlie the sweeping changes taking place within the energy industries:

- **Technology** is advancing at a rapid pace, reducing many of the costs and risks associated with the production and use of conventional and non-conventional energy resources. For example, recent technological developments have reduced significantly the costs of oil and gas exploration, and facilitated the production of resources in locations and in quantities previously deemed uneconomic. Similarly, fuel cell technologies are steadily improving and growing less expensive, heightening confidence that viable alternatives to conventional fossil fuel transportation technologies as well as major improvements in overall efficiency of use may become available in the next decade or two. Many key questions were addressed: What factors will determine whether or not new technologies are adopted? What will the nation's, and the world's, future research and development architecture look like? How will the science and technology roles of government, the private sector, and universities evolve in upcoming decades?

- **The Environment** plays a more important role than ever as a driver of change in the energy industries. Significant areas of unique biological diversity are threatened with extinction, urban air quality in most of the developing world is badly deteriorating, and we are in the midst of a grand experiment to learn the climate effects of ever increasing atmospheric concentrations of carbon dioxide. Yet the United States and other major economies continue to devote significant expenditure to what may be the least cost-effective environmental measures. The Forum considered several environment-related energy questions: How can we establish environmental priorities on a global basis? How do we determine the appropriate goal for CO_2 concentrations at the Kyoto Conference? What would be the likely economic effects of an agreement, or a failure to agree? How can our trade policies better account for environmental effects?

- **Market Structures** are changing rapidly in the energy industries, under pressure from the forces of deregulation, globalization, and free trade. In the U.S., the U.K., Australia, New Zealand, and several other countries, deregulation and privatization are introducing market competition to the electric utility sector, creating numerous entrepreneurial opportunities while, at the same time, stranding many previous investments and raising questions about the appropriate future role of government in these industries. Market forces are also contributing to the blurring of boundaries among energy industries, as oil, gas, coal, and electricity producers merge and partner with one another to form the energy conglomerates of the future. Key questions raised at the Forum regarding market structure included: How will U.S. and world energy markets evolve by 2020? How will perceptible demographic trends affect energy markets? What will energy companies look like? What regulatory structures will be appropriate in the future?

While each of these three drivers is significant, their interactions and feedbacks with one another heighten the uncertainties associated with the future of the energy industries. Moreover, all of these primary drivers play out in the context of politics at the global, regional, national, and sub-national levels. Geopolitical changes, such as the end of the Cold War, have obviously altered the relative importance of strategic versus economic policy considerations and fueled the processes of globalization and market liberalization. In similar fashion, technological changes have influenced geopolitics, for instance, by facilitating the growth and diversification of oil and gas supply, and by expanding nations' fuel options. With this dynamic political environment as its context, the 1997 Energy Policy Forum considered each of the three drivers described above from the perspective of the rapidly-changing energy industries.

Session 1:
The Geopolitics of Energy

While previous Forum meetings have sought to avoid politics as a primary theme, this year's participants made geopolitics a focal point of discussion, given the unprecedented changes around the globe that bear directly on the future of energy.

Regional Developments in Energy Politics

Recent developments across Latin America exemplify a trend toward democratization and liberal transformation of national political economies that is occurring around the world. In Venezuela, Chile, Columbia, and Brazil, public utility companies and other energy assets are on the road to privatization. This shift marks a reversal of the process of nationalization of energy assets in Latin America that began in the early 1970s; several nations, including Argentina, Bolivia, Brazil, Colombia, Peru, and Ecuador, have now unbundled, deregulated, and privatized their oil, gas, and electric utility industries to varying degrees. Many view these changes as an encouraging sign that markets are being invoked to reinforce newly-instituted democratic governance, citizen empowerment, and political stability in the region. In several nations, the growing flow of investment into upstream projects (estimated at $5 billion/year in Venezuela alone) is possibly the most convincing indicator of the sea changes in both industry and state structures that are

sweeping Latin America. Mexico and Venezuela, which together account for some 60% of the region's total petroleum production, merit particular attention for the reforms they have
initiated. The Mexican national oil company, PEMEX, a symbol
of the national patrimony since the early twentieth century, has
begun to liberalize elements of the downstream gas and petro-
chemical industries, with a view to divesting up to 49% of its
holdings in those subsectors. In Venezuela, efforts to expand
reserves and capacity have focused on market mechanisms, and
have sought private capital to reactivate and maximize oil
recovery from older fields, to use strategic association contracts
to produce once-unattractive extra heavy Orinoco crudes, and
to set up profit sharing arrangements to spur new discovery
and fresh capacity development. These developments are
viewed as harbingers of a bright energy, economic, and political future throughout Latin America.

Democratization, privatization of energy assets, and liberalization of Latin American markets have helped to reinvigorate
the region's energy industries by attracting large inflows of foreign investment and new technologies. Such developments,
while naturally of great regional significance, have far-reaching
geopolitical importance as well. These eventualities are due in
part to the fact that, with approximately 13% of the world's
total petroleum reserves, the Latin American region is a major
net exporter of petroleum and one that holds great potential
for further development. Some analysts estimate that Latin
American gas reserves, for example, are on the order of
350tcf—greater than any region but the Middle East.[1]

Capital inflows aiming to develop these resources, given the
optimistic outlooks for Latin America's petroleum reserves and
overall political economy, will contribute to the regionalization
of energy markets and to the diversification of petroleum supply, both of which are important emerging trends in the
geopolitics of energy. Even with intraregional demand for oil
and gas growing at an estimated 4% per year, reserve and production growth projections suggest that Latin America will
have an exportable surplus on the order of 7-8 million barrels

per day (mbd) over the next two decades. Nonetheless, many foreign investors continue to view Latin America as a risky environment, given its recent history of social, economic, and political turmoil. Thus the optimistic projections described above are predicated, to a large degree, on Latin America's future success in using its growing revenue streams to facilitate human development and to dampen the region's sharp income inequalities, which could fuel future social and political conflicts if unabated.

The figure below places emerging prospects in the petroleum industry in a global context. Although recent technological advances, democratization, and discoveries in Latin America and Central Asia have expanded the world's recoverable petroleum reserves, access to the majority of these resources is largely limited to state oil companies. Private international oil and gas companies, which have considerable market access and skills, are now focusing on production opportunities in smaller provinces where firms can retain more control over their investments.

FIGURE 1

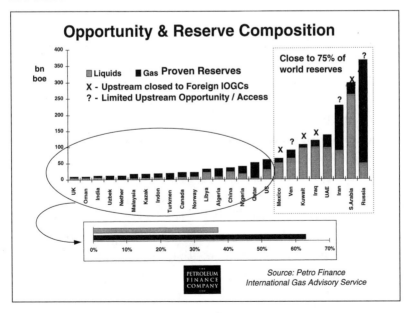

In contrast to the generally optimistic scenario that is unfolding in Latin America and elsewhere, political and economic developments in the Middle East give cause for caution and for the expectation of surprises in upcoming years. To the year 2000, the oil outlook for the Middle East appears stable, facilitated by a weak and divided OPEC and low world prices. In the medium- to long-term, however, the security of Middle Eastern petroleum supplies remains uncertain. While Middle East oil production accounts for nearly 30% of current world supply (some 20 mbd), its ability to serve as the world's swing producer appears to be weakening as excess capacity has declined from over 11 mbd a decade ago to just 3 mbd today. Demand growth around the world, particularly in Asia, has absorbed much of the excess production capacity that existed previously in the oil market. At the same time, the lack of political and economic reforms in the Middle East has precluded investors' access to many of the region's largest producer nations, thereby forestalling the region's ability to draw new, badly-needed capital and technology for modernization and development of the industry. The internal political situations of several Persian Gulf nations, notably Saudi Arabia, Kuwait, Iraq, and Bahrain, raise many questions regarding the possibility and magnitude of future supply interruptions. Given the tightening of the world oil market, a significant political disturbance in Saudi Arabia, for example, could leave the world market in a state of serious shortfall for some time. The domestic stability of the other Gulf producers is growing more precarious, since many of them have depleted their currency reserves to finance wars and defense spending and find themselves in serious financial straits. Complicating matters further are the region's demographic and social characteristics - rapid population growth, high unemployment, declining levels of social services, and growing popular dissatisfaction. The Gulf Cooperation Council has been largely unsuccessful, for that matter, in diversifying its member states' economies and broadening the opportunities available to their citizens.

On a more optimistic note, many Forum participants felt that the political and economic situations of Russia, Kazakhstan, and other former-Soviet states with large energy reserves could begin to stabilize in the near future, creating more favorable investment conditions there. Russian output could potentially climb from its current level of 4.5 mbd to 12 mbd over the next decade and a half. Similarly, Kazakhstan's output could grow to 2.5 mbd. Given low population growth rates across the Former Soviet Union, these additions to petroleum production could be available for export. Development of energy resources will depend in large measure on the maturation of the internal legal and political institutional structures in that region.

While current energy supply growth gives cause for optimism, important developments on the demand side give cause for concern. Demand in China alone, if current growth trends persist, could reach 20 mbd by the year 2020. In anticipation of future needs, the Chinese government has become a major bidder on upstream petroleum projects in key areas in Venezuela and Central Asia. Some Forum participants maintained that the development of transportation infrastructure in China and other rapidly-growing Asian countries would be among the principal drivers not only of fossil fuel demand and prices, but also of the viability of non-fossil fuel technologies in the future. Rapid petroleum demand growth in Asia could be an effective catalyst for alternative energy technology development, although it appears unlikely that such options will be serious contenders in the next ten years, given current prices and technology investments.

U.S. Policy and the Future of Energy

In light of the risks emerging in the Middle East and uncertainties associated with future petroleum production in Latin America and the Former Soviet Union, the West appears poorly prepared for likely and possible eventualities. While it is unclear how consequential a disruption of supply might be, the International Energy Agency appears insufficiently capable of coping with future crises of significant magnitude or duration. Moreover, the U.S. has alienated many of its allies and possibly compromised its position through its widespread use of economic sanctions as a foreign policy instrument. The full or partial sanctions in place against Iran, Iraq, Libya, Burma, and Indonesia could prove not only ineffective but detrimental to the U.S., if and when future energy crises arise. More broadly, the growing tide of U.S.-imposed economic sanctions raises questions concerning Washington's professed commitment to free trade and the extent to which the U.S. government will continue to wield sanctions as a weapon of choice in future foreign policy conflicts.

Within the U.S., the political risks associated with energy, while different from those in other regions, are considerable in their own right. For example, the recently-implemented Environmental Protection Agency regulations further constraining NO_x and fine particulate emissions have introduced important new uncertainties for energy companies. The sale of substantial portions of the U.S. Strategic Petroleum Reserve, in response to budgetary pressures, augments the nation's energy-related risks. However, some analysts maintain that the costs of developing and maintaining a petroleum reserve infrastructure would be likely to exceed those inflicted by future energy crises in any event. Those advocating the liquidation of petroleum reserves feel that price spikes may be a better means of managing crises in terms of economic efficiency, especially in deregulated and well-functioning energy markets. Potential economic efficiencies aside, however, others believe the distributional effects of price volatility could produce powerful political reactions and lead to subsequent governmental interventions in the market.

Despite the central role that politics plays in the global petroleum industry, many major oil and gas corporations may be insufficiently prepared to manage the political risks that will be essential to their future success. While companies are better equipped than ever to deal with the "below ground" risks of upstream oil and gas - the technological challenges of exploration and production—they are less adept at dealing with the "above ground" risks associated with negotiation, government relations, policy risks, and marketing in their core geographical areas. Following years of downsizing, streamlining, and cost-cutting in their management and operations, many companies have grown more skilled at *running* a business than they are at *doing* business. The latter set of skills will be especially important in the gas business, where the above ground/marketing risks are greater than in the oil business. U.S. companies, hamstrung by unilaterally-imposed sanctions on key countries, may be at a disadvantage across the board in some areas. Those best positioned to do well may be the independents, which historically have excelled at managing their upstream relationships. The ability to manage government and public relations, at home and abroad, will be among the most valuable talents in the future.

Session 2: Technology

In order to appreciate the extent to which technology is likely to have an impact on the energy industries over the next two decades, one need only look back at some of the major developments of the past twenty years. Significant advances have occurred in basic science, the impacts of which have been felt in virtually every area of energy technology including fossil fuels, efficiency, electricity generation, and alternatives such as fuel cells and solar technologies.

Public policy has been a major factor in energy technology, directly or indirectly, as environmental regulations have prompted the development of cleaner, more efficient technologies, while government research and development programs have yielded major advances such as gas turbine electricity generation. Principal forces of technological change in the energy industries at present include: the rapidly unfolding revolution in information, the full effects of which are currently inestimable; the worldwide currents of deregulation, competition, and market-based reforms which are fueling innovation, cost-reduction, and major industry restructuring; and the environmental, technological, and political challenges posed by the threat of global climate change. These forces in concert promise to craft an energy sector of vastly different technological form by the year 2020.

Technology: Key Findings

- Technology has the potential to produce — indeed, holds the key to — a wealthier and more environmentally benign world. It is especially important that the developing countries build their economies in ways that allow them to avoid, to the greatest extent possible, the "brown" phases through which the industrialized nations have passed.

- The relationship between technology and market structure is critical and requires further study and understanding. Technology is facilitating the development of global markets, yet technology policy in the future must be designed to respond to demand pull, rather than to initiate supply push as has often been its function in the past. In order to avoid supply push, the government's role in technology R&D in the future might best be limited to pre-competitive and basic research, allowing the private sector to listen and respond to customers as its principal driver.

- While markets may be the most effective and—at least currently—the most popular means of affecting technology choices, they may ignore important problems such as distributional equity, geopolitical concerns (e.g., dependence on unreliable partners) and—unless internalized—environmental considerations.

- In the light of global environmental concerns and energy demand growth projections, the potential advantages and disadvantages of nuclear energy technologies should be revisited and reconsidered thoroughly.

The Technological Challenge of Global Climate Change

The Framework Convention on Climate Change (FCCC), a treaty signed by over 150 nations at the Rio Earth Summit in 1992, aims to forestall the "atmospheric concentration of greenhouse gases at dangerous levels" which could, in turn, alter the earth's climate in undesirable and uncertain ways. Despite the FCCC's focus on the long-term concentrations of greenhouse gases in the atmosphere, much of the internationalal political debate around the climate change problem has revolved around the question of short-term (e.g., the next decade) greenhouse gas emissions rates. In what has become a highly polarized debate, the industrialized nations of the North—the largest historic and current emitters—are often portrayed by nations of the less-industrialized South as the source of the climate change problem and, thus, as those that ought to bear the high costs presumed to be associated with its solution. In contrast, Northern nations frequently point to the rapid rates of population and energy growth in industrializing nations, arguing that their own efforts to reduce emissions would be fruitless absent significant participation of the South.

In addition to fostering diplomatic discord, the emphasis on near-term greenhouse gas emissions may divert attention from significant opportunities to address the climate change problem and to spur the development of a new generation of advanced energy technologies at extremely low cost—below 1% of global GDP. Realizing this potential would require substantial improvements in fossil and alternative energy technologies, and would demand the creation of institutional mechanisms to reduce emissions whenever and wherever in the world it is least expensive to do so. If advanced, low- and non-carbon energy technologies were to become sufficiently efficient and cost competitive, the costs of atmospheric stabilization at higher-than-present levels of greenhouse gases could be reduced or eliminated altogether. Similarly, competition could greatly reduce the costs of enforcement, since the new energy technologies would serve as a basis for comparative advantage and national export.

Producing a new generation of non-carbon energy technologies would require significantly increased levels of investment in energy research and development (R&D) in the U.S. and other OECD nations and a credible, sustained commitment to public education and technology deployment. Yet, R&D is a classic example of underproduction due to market failure, despite the fact that it could be viewed as a "no regrets"

FIGURE 2

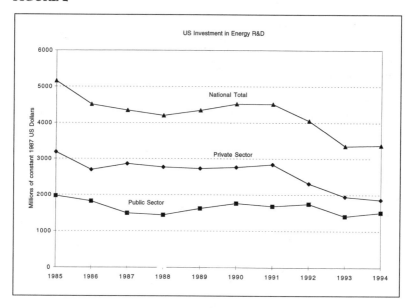

action. Although the costs of energy R&D would be more than recovered in the future, it appears unlikely that a concerted effort will be made to direct substantial new government or private investment toward the development of the new generation of technologies under any rationale. While this failure suggests that large competitive opportunities may be foregone, it also implies that nations might have to comply with international climate change obligations equipped only with the current generation of energy technologies. Compliance under these circumstances promises to be much more costly and far less effective in addressing the climate change problem.

Some Forum participants recommended fixing a "shadow price" on carbon—perhaps between $50 and $200/ton—which would help to stabilize atmospheric concentrations, and provide a market-based catalyst for research and development of new, low- or non-carbon energy technologies. Yet there is reason to question government's ability and willingness to intervene in this manner in circumstances increasingly characterized by market-based structures and rapid technological change.

Transportation Technology

Highway and airline traffic now account for nearly 85% of all transportation fuel consumption, of which petroleum accounts for some 90%. Current estimates reveal that this ratio is likely to remain steady through the year 2020, although transportation energy demand in the aggregate is growing rapidly worldwide. Due to the dramatic anticipated increases in transportation fuel use, considerations of fuel economy, total energy consumption, and engine emissions will be the dominant factors in future transportation vehicle and propulsion system designs. The next twenty-five years will be an intense, competitive, and technologically-driven period in a growing global transportation market.

Although the industrialized world is focusing on the production of vehicles that are far more energy efficient and far less polluting than those currently in use, the introduction of more technologically-advanced vehicles could escalate costs, effectively delaying their diffusion into the market. This dilemma poses a particularly great challenge in the industrializing world, where demand for transportation is outpacing the introduction of new and emission-reducing technologies.

In response to perceptible transportation challenges, an ambitious joint development effort, the Partnership for a New Generation of Vehicles (PNGV), has been mounted in the U.S. by the federal government's national laboratories, USCAR (a consortium of the "Big Three" auto makers to develop pre-competitive technologies), suppliers, and universities. Among the program's principal aims is the development of a mid-size sedan that achieves up to three times the fuel economy (80 mpg) of a comparable 1994 model year sedan, while maintaining or exceeding current levels of performance, value, size, and safety. As figure three shows, the goal of three times the current average fuel economy may be achieved via any of several technological pathways combining improvements in thermal efficiency, reductions in mass, and advances in regenerative braking.

FIGURE 3

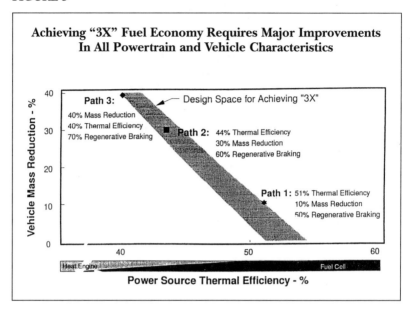

PNGV aims to produce concept vehicles by 2000, and production prototypes by 2004. In order to meet its ambitious targets, the program is investing in several new technologies that will increase thermal efficiency, and reduce vehicle weight and aerodynamic drag. Major areas of development include hybrid electric power trains; fuel cell electric power trains; mechanical and electro-chemical energy storage devices; electronic power control systems; regenerative braking; hydrogen storage; zeolite catalysis of emissions; ultra light weight materials; and lower rolling resistance tires.

Increasing environmental concerns—particularly efforts to reduce greenhouse gas emissions—could play a large role in increasing the viability of non-carbon, and low- or zero-emissions transportation technologies in the next two decades. Proton exchange fuel cell vehicles, given high rates of efficiency, fast refueling time, and long range, could present an attractive alternative to conventional fossil fuel technologies.

Current costs and limited refueling infrastructure present the most significant barriers to the widespread use of fuel cells in vehicles. Even though fuel cell costs are declining rapidly, their production costs are still prohibitive since they are largely hand-constructed in the laboratory by research scientists and engineers. If mass production were to become viable, one participant predicted, production costs could be reduced to a level that would allow fuel cells to compete with conventional technologies. Additionally, since one estimate of the cost of developing a hydrogen infrastructure for a fuel cell vehicle fleet is approximately $500 per vehicle, infrastructure costs may not be a significant long-term barrier to their adoption.

Energy and Technology in the Industrializing World

The nations of the industrializing world present some of the largest energy challenges and opportunities. While much of the discussion at the Energy Policy Forum concerned technology and market trends in OECD countries, it is important to note that the majority of the world's energy demand growth is occurring in industrializing nations, and much of that growth now relies upon old technologies and abundant, but dirty, coal resources. Examining emerging trends in the industrializing world helps to place the discussions of OECD energy concerns in a broader, global context. As one speaker noted, the industrialized world's strong emphasis on carbon emissions tends to overshadow the environmental and climate-related implications of rising methane emissions and deforestation rates in much of the global South. Trends in the South, if unabated, might easily subsume the best efforts of the North to apply new technologies to their own energy and environmental problems.

Despite the fact that nearly two-thirds of humanity still has no access to electricity, and despite growing climate concerns, nuclear energy technologies receive little serious consideration as a future means of meeting the industrializing world's burgeoning energy needs. Although expansion of nuclear power is not currently an option in the U.S., this is not the case globally. Even though concerns regarding the proliferation of nuclear materials, waste disposal, and safety persist, the envi-

ronmental merits of nuclear power may demand its consideration in developing nations. Many Forum participants felt that
there should be a comprehensive reexamination of the role of
nuclear power and its potential to contribute to the world's
energy future. The Forum, however, was not structured to allow
that comprehensive review.

Energy Technology: Policy Considerations

The achievement of a new generation of energy technologies over the next two decades will depend upon the continued
existence of a world class innovation infrastructure in the U.S.
Several recent historic developments, such as the end of the
Cold War and the globalization of markets, have called into
question the rationale behind the nation's public R&D infrastructure. Yet many Forum participants felt that a new energy
strategy aimed at deploying the next generation of advanced
energy technologies could only succeed if the nation's R&D
infrastructure were safeguarded. The rapid developments
in, and linkages between, technology areas suggest that the
rewards of public R&D investments are likely to be substantial,
albeit hard to foresee. Since the pace of technological change
is accelerating rapidly, the value of the various components of
the nation's R&D infrastructure may be greater than ever.
While there may be a temptation to dismantle parts of the R&D
establishment to reduce costs and eliminate budget deficits,
such actions might prove shortsighted. As one participant
noted, "intelligent tinkering means keeping all the parts."

Session 3: Environment

The relationships between energy, the economy, and the environment are increasingly intimate in the minds of business leaders, government officials, and the public at large. In part, this growing intimacy is due to the emergence of major environmental issues, such as global climate change, that have drawn direct linkages between energy use and possible adverse environmental impacts on a global scale.

Also, at the regional, national, and local levels, energy use is now commonly associated with air quality concerns, and has served as the impetus behind a rising tide of regulatory activity in the U.S. and around the world. Recently-proposed changes to EPA's source-performance standards for emissions of NOx and particulate matter from fossil fuel power plants underscore the environmental and regulatory challenges now facing the energy industries. They provided a timely backdrop for the Energy Policy Forum's discussion of the evolving relationship between energy and the environment in an era of deregulation, market-based mechanisms, and heightened global environmental awareness.

Broadening the Environmental Context

In recent decades, the world has learned a lot about the relationships between natural and human systems and about pri-

The Environment: Key Findings

- Public environmental awareness and support for environmental protection and enhancement is real and growing ever-stronger worldwide.

- Much of the planet's biological diversity is more threatened than ever.

- Possible global climate change presents many pressing challenges. Among these is the need for an energy system that is ecologically and economically sustainable. Any globally sustainable energy system should maximize the roles of market mechanisms and incentives; governments' roles should be limited to the establishment of the market structure and objectives and the enforcement of "rules of the game."

- While there is disagreement on the rate of change and the appropriateness of mitigative actions in the short term, climactic effects may be reasonably posited based on the cumulative levels of atmospheric greenhouse gas concentrations, rather than on emissions rates *per se*.

- Some climate change mitigation is occurring through the increasing electrification of energy. There is the potential for further mitigation through the continued electrification of transportation systems; although the associated costs are uncertain, they need not be prohibitively high.

- Although the industrialized nations are making progress with regard to climate change mitigation and greenhouse gas abatement, this progress will soon be overshadowed by the rapid growth in developing country emissions. The industrialized countries should encourage and facilitate the deployment of advanced, efficient energy technologies in the developing world and should take greater advantage of joint implementation arrangements.

- Investments in research, development, and deployment (RD&D) yield high returns economically and environmentally. Establishment of a funding mechanism for RD&D, supported perhaps by a BTU tax or a wire charge, merits consideration.

- Current environmental program priorities are designed largely to respond to short term problems that are less important than longer term issues, which are receiving inadequate attention.

oritizing and focusing efforts to protect the most unique eco-
logical systems and habitats of the planet. Some of the satellite
monitoring and management activities of the World Wildlife
Fund (WWF) and others help to illustrate the evolution in
human understanding of the natural world that has, in turn,
broadened the context for environmental protection. For
example, WWF has identified some 200 "ecoregions"—marine,
aquatic, and terrestrial ecosystems that are the most outstanding examples of the earth's eighteen major habitats and eco-
logical systems. Prioritizing the regions of the world in this way
may enable governments, businesses, and people to conserve
the most representative examples of biodiversity and make less
daunting the task of saving the planet.

Despite such expansions of human understanding, however,
the conditions of many ecosystems around the world are continuing to deteriorate and many species have been lost recently. This failure points to the importance of integrating social
considerations and social science knowledge into environmental assessments. Protecting the environment and promoting
sustainability, for instance, may be best served by promoting
women's health and education in less industrialized nations, or
by addressing the complex dynamics of human demographic
trends around the world, rather than by managing species and
ecosystems per se. If this analysis is correct, it contributes greatly to humanity's ability to set priorities for environmental protection and long-term sustainability. With regard to energy
planning and the future, however, it also raises difficult questions about energy-environment linkages. The most significant
is likely to be climate change effects on these critical ecoregions, but other questions are persistent as well. What, for
example, might biomass energy, distributed utility technologies, and future energy infrastructure development imply for
ecosystemic and species survival? Also, as market mechanisms
and market culture become more prominent as elements of
decision making, the question of how to represent social, environmental, and other non-market values remains crucial.

Trade and the Environment

The accelerating phenomena of globalization and market capitalism have raised new questions concerning the nexus between trade and the environment. Many Forum participants view the ongoing expansion of free trade as something of a mixed bag from an environmental standpoint. On the one hand, the growth in private sector investment has generated unprecedented levels of economic growth, opportunity, and prosperity, alleviating the environmental impacts of poverty. Furthermore, the lowering of trade barriers and deregulation of key industries in many countries has spurred competition and introduced new economic incentives for efficiency in many areas.

On the other hand, free trade and trading regimes such as the North American Free Trade Agreement (NAFTA) may have had serious detrimental impacts on the environment. In addition to bringing substantial economic benefits, particularly to Mexico, NAFTA's passage also brought perceptible declines in environmental quality, as companies opened or expanded operations in the Mexican border zone, where less stringent environmental regulations and enforcement confer a competitive advantage over production in the U.S. In fact, many former advocates of free trade have adopted more protectionist stances in view of the environmental impacts that have resulted from free trade regimes such as NAFTA and the World Trade Organization.

While many of the environmental problems associated with free trade regimes such as NAFTA may be endemic to free trade, some may be attributed to the failure of members to meet their commitments under such agreements. For example, the U.S. has promised nearly $8 billion of support that has not yet materialized for environmental management efforts in the border zone. Since governments' discretionary budgets—in the U.S. and many other countries—are declining, the prospects for resource commitments to meet such obligations are slim. Thus, it was asserted that, if free trade and sustainability are both to proceed, new modes of operation that unite these two goals must be devised. An industrial ecology approach to free trade, centering on economic and environmental efficiencies, might offer a starting point. Eliminating the need to constantly "clean up after ourselves" would be a sensible strategy from both a business and an ecological perspective.

Environmental Policy and the Future

On an optimistic note, the world has learned much from its mistakes in environmental policy-making over the past two decades. As a result, a transformation is occurring, driven by still-growing levels of public concern for and awareness of the environment and by the refinement of policy tools available to decision makers. In the U.S. and elsewhere, there is a steady movement away from the command and control policies of the past, which have proven costly and ineffective in many cases. Policies increasingly incorporate market mechanisms that provide industry and consumers with economic and fiscal incentives to reduce waste and pollution.

The acid rain cap-and-trade system illustrates the potential effectiveness of blending of policy goals and market mechanisms. The reduction of SO_2 emissions in the U.S. is currently proceeding 38% ahead of schedule as a result of the incentives provided to innovators and early achievers in industry. The system allows the market to determine technological compliance options, penalizes environmental laggards, and subsidizes environmental leaders. Forum participants expressed the hope that similar mechanisms might be used as a means of reducing greenhouse gas emissions, should binding reductions be agreed upon in upcoming international climate negotiations.

Several participants expressed serious concerns that emissions reduction commitments might be made in Kyoto in the absence of a long-term strategy for the development of a new generation of energy technologies, and in the absence of reciprocal commitments on the part of developing countries. Since developing nations will account for nearly 85% of the growth

FIGURE 5

Carbon Emissions from Fossil Fuels, Billion Metric Tons

	1995	2015	
World	6.24	9.70	(+3.46)
United States	1.42	1.80	(+0.38)
OECD (Incl. U.S.; Excl. Mexico, Eastern Europe, South Korea)	3.05	3.89	(+0.84)
Eastern Europe/Former Soviet Union	0.89	1.25	(+0.36)
China	0.82	1.84	(+1.02)
India	0.22	0.49	(+0.27)
Entire Developing World (Incl. Mexico)	2.29	4.56	(+2.27)

Source: U.S. Energy Information Administration.

in greenhouse gas emissions over the next twenty years, a policy course that does not address this growth, and worldwide demographic trends in general, seems destined to be both costly and ineffective in dealing with climate change. Still, other participants expressed concern about the lack of broad public understanding of the issue, which, when combined with persistent scientific uncertainties, suggests that the U.S. may not have the requisite political support to implement the accord that may result from the Kyoto negotiations. Many participants thought a serious public discourse on these matters was urgently required.

Session 4: Market Structures

All of the energy industries are now in the course of rapid transformation propelled by a host of domestic and international forces. The lessons learned through government regulation of energy over the past few decades in OECD countries has prompted a tide of deregulation and the introduction of market forces and competition to unprecedented degrees. At the same time, in several Latin American countries and throughout the Former Soviet Union and Eastern Europe, for example, sweeping political and economic changes have introduced democratic governance and market capitalism and opened up major new opportunities for energy investors.[2] (Underlying these trends is the more universal current of globalization, a process fueled by advances in telecommunications and information technologies, opening and integration of markets around the world, and a growing level of awareness of interdependencies among societies.)

More regional and localized drivers are also at play, propelling change in the electric utility industry perhaps most of all. For example, in the United Kingdom, deregulation of electric power has been prompted largely by Conservative political ideology. In New Zealand, pressures for greater economic efficiency appear to have provided the strongest impetus for deregulation and competition in the power industry. The needs for new capital and international investment have compelled lib-

31

Market Structures: Key Findings

- Competition in the electric utility industry will continue to accelerate in the U.S. These dynamics will compel firms in the industry to make the transition from integrated monopoly to market competitor quickly. There will be no resisting the forces of technological change, liberalization, and globalization. In developing countries, the introduction of market forces to the energy industries will proceed more slowly.

- Developing countries may have opportunities to "leapfrog" the industrialized countries by using advanced technologies and methods proven most effective and efficient in energy, environmental, and economic terms. Industrialized nations should seek to facilitate this.

- Market boundaries will continue to blur and energy services will grow increasingly commoditized.

- Although market mechanisms will be increasingly important in the future of the electric power industry, government will still play a vital oversight role, for instance, in ensuring that there are no barriers to entry and that there is no anti-trust behavior.

---

eralization and reform in many parts of Latin America and Asia. These proximate causes may be seen as regional manifestations, or second order effects, of the larger global-scale forces of change, as well as contributors to the global currents.

As a result of these shifts, the energy company of the year 2020 will bear little resemblance to its counterpart of the present. Boundaries between oil, gas, electric utilities, water and telecommunications companies will continue to blur as the variety of new business opportunities and new entrants grows. While traditional structures may persist in selected markets and geographic regions (e.g., China and India), in general the industries will become increasingly fragmented, and oriented toward providing services in specific market niches. At the same time, as technology advances, product lifecycles will grow shorter and assets will become secondary to knowledge, flexibility, and adaptability as determinants of success in an ever more volatile and dynamic environment.

Directions of Change: Two Scenarios to 2020

Liberalization, globalization, and technology are the primary global forces that are shaping the future. While observers may differ with regard to the "end states" to which these currents might be carrying the world, there is no denying their existence or their magnitude. Under these circumstances, then, it is meaningless to discuss a "business as usual" scenario since there is no alternative to large scale change. It is more useful to examine the nature of change and to envision the social and institutional structures that might be the most successful in this context. The two alternative scenarios described below, which were developed by Royal Dutch/Shell, offer greatly divergent, yet equally plausible depictions of the future and of the attributes of a successful future society.

"Just Do It"

In the first scenario, success comes to those who harness the latest innovations in technology to identify and capitalize on fast-moving opportunities in a world of hypercompetition, customization, dematerialization, self-reliance, and ad hoc, informal networking. This world allows the fullest expression of individual creativity and offers a wide stage for exploring new ways of doing business, solving problems, and seizing "bubbles of value"—highly profitable, highly-perishable business opportunities. In a "Just Do It" world, successful companies and societies stress innovation and individual initiative, and tolerate a high degree of creative anarchy. Working groups come together to solve specific problems and dissolve when the task is done. For the most part, it is a self-organizing world in which groups are conscious of themselves and their own organizing principles.

"Just Do It" suggests a growing consensus that the private sector is more successful than government in managing such services as pension schemes, utilities, and educational systems. National governments shrink as citizens insist on solving problems at the local level, just as they do in business, where power is delegated close to the customer. People who are uncomfortable with the relentless pace of change feel alienated from the economy and the political process, especially since the drivers of change have narrowed the scope of practical political debate at the same time as information technology has increased the number of people directly involved in it.

"Just Do It" has far-reaching implications for the energy industries. First, it suggests that competition and the rapid pace of technological change will drive an ever closer integration of information technology in all aspects of energy production and consumption. Expert systems and control technologies will continually improve the efficiency and quality of service and assist companies both upstream in discovery and production and downstream in customer characterization. Consumers will also benefit from the development of "intelligent appliances" and other products that improve efficiency and performance.

Second, the virtual nature of the "Just Do It" society suggests the dematerialization and decentralization of the economy, as people work from home and engage increasingly in knowledge-based business, and rely more heavily on advanced telecommunications technologies for their regular interactions. These patterns of work, interaction, and travel imply considerably different patterns of energy use from those of the present.

Finally, "Just Do It" embodies a market in which there is no competitive equilibrium, and where the boundaries between the traditional energy industries become blurred as gas, oil, and electricity companies, service providers, entrepreneurs, and even companies in other industries are able to enter the energy market. Demand is uncertain, volatile, and cyclical, and stranded assets present a large and chronic problem.

"Da Wo" ("Big Me")

In the second scenario, countries and companies discover that success calls for a committed investment in relationships, where relationships of trust and the enabling role of government provide the long-term strategic advantage. In this world, Asia already has the advantage because its societies and businesses are at home in a world in which the individual—the "small me"—understands that individual welfare is inextricably linked to the welfare of the whole—*"Da Wo"* ("Big Me"). In successful *"Da Wo"* societies, networks of trust substitute for the web of legal contracts and other expensive transaction costs associated with doing business in the West. An even greater strategic advantage lies in the approach to the workforce. People respond to the sense of security and cultural identity that these societies provide, and are able to give more in return.

Yet, *"Da Wo"* is not just a simple extension of the "Asian model," although it embodies many of the same values; nor is it a welfare-oriented world. On the contrary, the duties associ-

FIGURE 6

The Learning Scenarios

Just Do It!	Themes	*Da Wo*
Individualism	Themes	Cohesion
Libertarianism	Politics	Governments matter
Hypercompetition	Economics	Increasing returns
Dematerialisation	Energy	Sustained growth
Bubbles of Value	Business	Being Asian
Blurring boundaries		Balancing stakeholder pressures
Rapid technological change		Building long-term advantage

ated with cohesion are significant, and sanctions on free riders are severe. The emphasis is on responsibilities, not rights. This scenario reflects a new synthesis between the social and cultural values of cohesion and the maverick, impersonal drivers of change. A model for this synthesis might combine particular features of such countries as Chile, Singapore, and Switzerland. Individualistic societies in a "*Da Wo*" world continue to invent many new technologies, but they fail to profit from these because of internal fragmentation and because they lack the ability and will to develop the necessary long-term vision and commitment to innovation, research, and development.

"*Da Wo*" suggests rapid growth in the energy industries, driven largely by high rates of economic growth in Asia, which accounts for nearly half of the incremental oil demand to the year 2020. The steadily increasing demand pressure heralds not only a renaissance in the conventional energy industries, but also the increasing commercial viability of alternative fuels (including biomass, wind, and solar PV), as fossil fuel prices rise.

Changing Structures in the Global Power Industry

In the electric utility sector, global forces such as growing capital flows, unbundling, consolidation, and customer choice, are driving the industry toward a competitive end state. While more than 50% of the world's electric utilities remain integrated monopolies, and only 4% are competitive businesses, by 2007 the reverse is likely to be true. The value creation potential inherent in these dynamics has been estimated at around $150 billion annually worldwide.

The increasing competitive intensity in the global power industry is also placing enormous pressure on project returns. Winning projects are viewed as those that promise in the vicinity of a 13%-16% return to capital. At the same time, the combination of skills required for success is evolving. Companies can no longer operate as power developers, but must view themselves as business builders with a keen understanding of

FIGURE 7-A

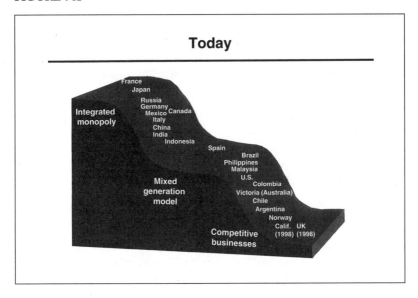

FIGURE 7-B

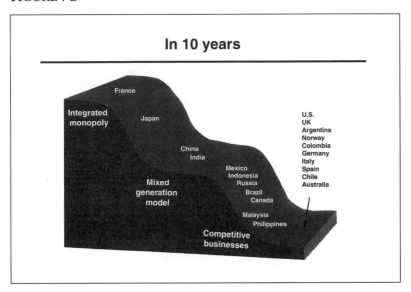

their local, regional, and global contexts in addition to their technical skills. Thus, some of the greatest challenges that power companies will face in the future will be those of attracting and retaining key people with area knowledge and expertise, organizing international operations, and establishing alliances and partnerships in key regions and industry sectors. The future industry will have a small handful of successful global operators, perhaps 15-20 larger players in multiple regional markets, a complex network of regional and interregional alliances, and countless local and regional service providers.

The structure of the U.S. electric utility industry in particular is a major concern of many Forum participants. As deregulation proceeds and competition is introduced, many key players in the industry appear to be adept at turning their current positions to their advantage. For example, many believe that utilities have become skilled in manipulating the environmental regulatory process for market advantage. By the same token, many new entrants are seeking to perpetuate imperfect energy markets on which they rely for their success and continued existence.

The question is whether or not an efficient, competitive industry will emerge from the clash of interests outlined above. Significant concerns were raised, although not elaborately discussed, about the adequacy of ISOs and open-access transmission regimes, at both the state and federal levels, in preventing market dominance.

Footnotes

[1] Recent reports suggest, however, that gas discoveries in the Caspian Sea may give that region claim to the largest known gas endowment in the world.

[2] See: *Dilemmas of Utility Restructuring in Central and Eastern Europe,* a report of The Aspen Institute's workshop in Krakow, Poland, May 7-10, 1997 (available from The Aspen Institute, Washington, DC.).

Forum Participants

P. J. Adam
Chairman and Chief
Executive Officer
Black & Veatch
8400 Ward Parkway
PO Box 8405
Kansas City, MO 64114

John A. Anderson
Executive Director
ELCON
1333 H St., NW
West Tower, 8th Floor
Washington, DC 20005

Richard E. Ayres
Partner
Howrey & Simon
1299 Pennsylvania Ave., NW
Washington, DC 20004-2402

Merribel S. Ayres
President
Lighthouse Energy Group,
LLC
1001 N. 19th St., Ste 1950
Arlington, VA 22209

The Honorable Vicky A. Bailey
Commissioner
Federal Energy Regulatory
Commission
888 First Street, NE
Suite 11B
Washington, DC 20426

Henri-Claude Bailly
Managing Director
Hagler Bailly Consulting,
Inc.
1530 Wilson Blvd.
Suite 900
Arlington, VA 22209

Richard E. Balzhiser
President Emeritus
Electric Power Research
Institute
P.O. Box 10412
3412 Hillview Avenue
Palo Alto, CA 94304

Roger A. Berliner
Managing Partner
Brady & Berliner
1225 19th Street, NW
Suite 800
Washington, DC 20036

Ellen Berman
President
Electric Utility Restructuring
Forum
Consumer Energy Council
of America Research
Foundation
2000 L Street, NW
Suite 802
Washington, DC 20036

Peter D. Blair
Executive Director
Sigma Xi, The Scientific
Research Society
P.O. Box 13975
99 Alexander Drive
Research Triangle Park, NC
27709

John E. Bryson
Chairman of the Board and
CEO
Southern California Edison
Company
2244 Walnut Grove Avenue
P.O. Box 800
Rosemead, CA 91770

George Lee Butler
President
Kiewit Energy Group
1000 Kiewit Plaza
Omaha, NE 68131-3374

Paul J. Cardenas
Pacific Enterprises
555 W. 5th Street - ML29H2
Los Angeles, CA 90013

Collis P. Chandler, Jr.
Chairman of the Board
& CEO
The Chandler Company
475 17th Street
Suite 1000
Denver, CO 80202

John F. Clarke
Manager
Public Sector Energy
Accounts
Battelle, Pacific Northwest
National Laboratory
370 L'Enfant Promenade
901 D Street, SW, Suite 900
Washington, DC 20024

Frost Cochran
Managing Partner
Energy Asset Management,
LLC
250 Montgomery St.
Suite 1600
San Franciso, CA 94104

Greg Conlon
President
California Public Utilities
Commission
State Building—
505 VanNess Ave.
San Francisco, CA 94102

Chester L. Cooper
Deputy Director
Emerging Technologies
Battelle, Pacific Northwest
    National Laboratory
901 D Street, SW, Suite 900
Washington, DC 20024

Benjamin S. Cooper
Executive Director
Association of Oil Pipelines
1101 Vermont Ave., NW
Suite 604
Washington, DC 20005

Loren C. Cox
Associate Director
MIT Center for Energy &
    Environmental Policy
    Research
350 Belaire Court
Punta Gorda, FL 33950

Charles B. Curtis
Hogan & Hartson
555 13th Street, NW
Washington, DC 20004-1109

Wilfried Czernie
Senior General Manager
Ruhrgas A.G.
Huttropstrasse 60 - D-45138
    Essen
Federal Republic of
    Germany

Charles J. DiBona
President
American Petroleum
    Institute
1220 L Street, NW
Washington, DC 20005

William E. Dickenson
President
Putnam, Hayes & Bartlett,
    Inc.
1776 I Street, NW
Washington, DC 20006

J.W. Dickey
Chief Operating Officer
Tennessee Valley Authority
400 West Summit Hill Drive
Knoxville, TN 37902

Paul Dragoumis
President
Paul Dragoumis Associates,
    Inc.
P.O. Box 5
Cabin John, MD 20818

Theodore R. Eck
Chief Economist
Amoco Corporation
MC 2905A
200 East Randolph
Chicago, IL 60601

Patricia Eckert
Strategic Partner
Deloitte & Touche
    Consulting Group
56 CASA
San Francisco, CA 94123

James A. Edmonds
Technical Leader, Economics
    Programs
Battelle - Pacific Northwest
    Laboratories
901 D Street, SW
Suite 900
Washington, DC 20024

Juan Eibenschutz
Subdirector de Distribucion
Y Comercializacion
Luz Y Fuerza Del Centro
Melchor Ocampo 171-8
11379 Mexico, D.F.

Dr. Herman Franssen
President
International Energy
Associates, Inc.
4515 Willard Ave., Apt. 903S
Chevy Chase, MD 20815

Robert W. Fri
Director
National Museum of Natural
History
10th and Constitution Aves.,
NW
Room 421
Washington, DC 20560

William Fulkerson
Senior Fellow
Joint Institute for Energy &
Environment
600 Henley Street
Suite 34
Knoxville, TN 37996-4138

Robert W. Gee
Commissioner
The Public Utility
Commission of Texas
1701 N. Congress Ave.
Austin, TX 78701

John H. Gibbons
Assistant to the President for
Science & Technology
Executive Office of the
President
The White House
OEB-424
Washington, DC 20500

Craig G. Goodman
Senior Vice President, Law,
Regulation and Public
Policy
Equitable Resources,
Incorporated
3333 K Street, Suite 425
Washington, DC 20007

Robert L. Hirsch
Consultant
The Energytechnology
Collaborative, Inc.
4066 Mansion Drive, NW
Washington, DC 20007

William W. Hogan
Thornton Bradshaw
Professor of Public Policy
and Management
Kennedy School of
Government
Harvard University
79 John F. Kennedy Street
Cambridge, MA 02138

Sheila S. Hollis
Senior Partner
Metzger, Hollis, Gordon &
Mortimer
Attorneys at Law
1275 K Street, NW
Suite 1000
Washington, DC 20005

Paul Holtberg
Group Manager
Baseline/Gas Resource
    Analytical Center
Gas Research Institute
1331 Pennsylvania Avenue,
    NW
Suite 730 North
Washington, DC 20004-1703

H.M. Hubbard
President and CEO (Ret)
PICHTR
3245 Newland Street
Wheat Ridge, CO 80033

Toshio Inoue
Chief Economist
Cosmo Oil Co., Ltd.
1-1-1, Shibaura, Minato-ku
Tokyo 105, Japan

Ira H. Jolles
Sr. Vice President and
    General Counsel
General Public Utilities
    Corporation, Inc.
100 Interpace Parkway
Parsippany, NJ 07054

Trevor O. Jones
Chairman of the Board
Echlin, Inc.
Orangewood Place, Suite 450
3690 Orange Place
Beachwood, OH 44122

Jack L. King
President, Controlled System
    Division
Scientific Atlanta, Inc.
4311 Communications Drive
Norcross, GA 30093

Wilfrid L. Kohl
Director, Energy &
    Environment Program
Johns Hopkins University
SAIS
1619 Massachusetts Avenue,
    NW
Washington, DC 20036

Fred Krupp
Executive Director
Environmental Defense
    Fund
257 Park Avenue South
New York, NY 10010

Tom Kuhn
President
Edison Electric Institute
701 Pennsylvania Avenue,
    NW
Washington, DC 20004-2696

Lester Lave
Professor of Economics
Carnegie Mellon University
Graduate School of
    Industrial Administration
Pittsburgh, PA 15213

Kenneth L. Lay
Chairman and CEO
Enron Corp.
P.O. Box 1188
Houston, TX 77251-1188

P. Barrie Leay
Executive Director
ESANZ
Eagle Technology House
150-154 Willis Street
PO Box 1017
Wellington, New Zealand

Joseph L. LeGasse
Executive Adviser to the
CEO
Cinergy Corp.
221 East Fourth Street
Atrium 30
Cincinnati, OH 45201

Henry R. Linden
Director, Energy and Power
Center
Illinois Institute of
Technology
PH-135
10 West 33rd Street
Chicago, IL 60616-3793

Ian Lindsay
Secretary General
World Energy Council
34 St. James's Street
London SW1A IHD
England

Amory B. Lovins
Director of Research and
Vice President
Rocky Mountain Institute
1739 Snowmass Creek Road
Old Snowmass, CO 81654-
9199

Christopher D. Maloney
Vice President and General
Manager
UNICOM Resources, Inc.
One First National Plaza
34th Floor
10 South Dearborn
Chicago, IL 60603

Jan W. Mares
EOP Group
1725 Desales Street, NW
Washington, DC 20036

Robert Marritz
Publisher
The Electricity Journal &
Daily
1501 Western Avenue
Suite 100
Seattle, WA 98101

Dr. I. S. Mishari
Vice President for Corporate
Planning
Saudi Aramco Services Co.
Room 3406 Administration
Building
Box 5000, Dhahran 31311
Saudi Arabia

Nancy C. Mohn
Director, Commercial
Analysis
ABB Power Plant Systems
2000 Day Hill Rd
Windsor, CT 06095-0500

Prof. M. Granger Morgan
Head, Dept. of Engineering
and Public Policy
Carnegie-Mellon University
Schenley Park
Pittsburgh, PA 15213

Leo F. Mullin
Vice Chairman
Commonwealth Edison
Company
P.O. Box 767
Chicago, IL 60690-0767

Gary Nakarado
Technical Director, Utility
    Programs
National Renewable Energy
    Laboratory
1617 Cole Boulevard, 17-3
Golden, CO 80401

William A. Nitze
Assistant Administrator
Office of International
    Activities
Environmental Protection
    Agency
Mail Code 2610
401 M Street, SW
Washington, DC 20460

Anthony S. H. Norton
Manager, Strategy Division of
    Corporate Planning
Exxon Corporation
5959 Las Colinas Avenue
Irving, TX 75039

Joan Ogden
Center for Energy &
    Environmental Studies
Princeton University
Princeton, NJ 08544

Dana Orwick
Program Director Emeritus
The Aspen Institute
6004 Winnebago Road
Bethesda, MD 20816

Alirio Parra
Senior Advisor
Centre for Global Energy
    Studies
14 Selwood Terraace
London SW7 3QN England

D. Louis Peoples
Vice Chairman and Chief
    Executive Officer
Orange and Rockland
    Utilities, Inc.
One Blue Hill Plaza, 21st
    Floor
Pearl River, NY 10965

John B. Phillips
Executive Director
California Energy Coalition
1540 South Coast Highway
Suite #204
Laguna Beach, CA 92681

Howard W. Pifer
Chairman
Putnam, Hayes & Bartlett,
    Inc.
One Memorial Drive
Cambridge, MA 02142

W. Arthur Porter
President and CEO
Houston Advanced Research
    Center
4800 Research Forest Dr.
The Woodlands, TX 77381

Paul R. Portney
President & Senior Fellow
Resources for the Future
1616 P Street, NW
Washington, DC 20036

Roger Rainbow
Vice President, Global
    Business Environment
Shell International Limited
Shell Centre
London SE1 7NA
United Kingdom

William K. Reilly
Founder & Chairman
Aqua International Partners
600 California Street
Suite 1850
San Francisco, CA 94108-
2704

John A. Riggs
Director
Program on Energy, the
Environment and
the Economy,
The Aspen Institute
1333 New Hampshire Ave.,
NW
Suite 1070
Washington, DC 20036

Ellen Roy
Senior Vice President
Intercontinental Energy
Corp.
350 Lincoln Place
Hingham, MA 02043

Paul Runci
Research Scientist
Battelle, Pacific Northwest
Laboratory
901 D Street, SW
Suite 900
Washington, DC 20024

Roger W. Sant
Chairman
The AES Corporation
1001 North 19th Street
Arlington, VA 22209

The Honorable Donald Santa, Jr.
Commissioner
Federal Energy Regulatory
Commission
888 First Street, NE
Washington, DC 20426

James R. Schlesinger
Lehman Brothers, Inc.
800 Connecticut Ave., NW
Suite 1200
Washington, DC 20006

Robert N. Schock
Acting Associate Director for
Energy Programs
Lawrence Livermore
National Laboratory
P.O. Box 808 - L640
7000 East Avenue
Livermore, CA 94551

John Shlaes
Executive Director
Global Climate Coalition
1331 Pennsylvania Ave., NW
Suite 1500 - North Lobby
Washington, DC 20004

Les Silverman
Director
McKinsey & Company
1101 Pennsylvania Avenue,
NW, #700
Washington, DC 20004

James M. Speyer
Managing Director
Putnam, Hayes & Bartlett,
Inc.
1776 I Street, NW
Washington, DC 20006

Irwin Stelzer
Director, Regulatory Policy
  Studies
American Enterprise
  Institute
1150 17th Street, NW
Washington, DC 20036

William D. Stevens
President & Chief Operating
  Officer
Mitchell Energy &
  Development Corp.
P.O. Box 4000
The Woodlands, TX 77387-
  4000

Ikuro Sugawara
General Manager
Japan National Oil Corp.
1750 New York Ave.,
  NW,Suite 335
Washington, DC 20006

John E. Treat
Vice President
Booz•Allen & Hamilton
101 California Street,
  Ste. 3300
San Francisco, CA 94111

F. William Valentino
President
New York State Energy
  Research & Development
  Authority
Corporate Plaza West
286 Washington Avenue
  Extension
Albany, NY 12203-6399

Andrew P. Varley
Senior Vice President
American Electric Power
1 Riverside Plaza
Columbus, OH 43215

Clinton A. Vince, Esq.
Co-Chairman
Verner, Liipfert, Bernhard,
  McPherson & Hand
901 15thStreet, NW,Suite 700
Washington, DC 20005

Susan OMalley Wade
Senior Associate
Program on Energy, the
  Environment, and
  the Economy,
The Aspen Institute
1333 New Hampshire Ave,
  NW, Ste. 1070
Washington, DC 20036

Dennis Wamsted
Executive Editor
The Energy Daily
627 National Press Building
529 14th Street, NW
Washington, DC 20045

J. Robinson West
Petroleum Finance
  Corporation
1300 Connecticut Ave., NW
Suite 800
Washington, DC 20036

Andrew W. Williams
Group Vice President
Energy, Market Policy &
    Development
Potomac Electric Power
    Company
1900 Pennsylvania Avenue,
    NW
Washington, DC 20068

Mason Willrich
Chairman
Energy Works
P.O. Box 50907
Palo Alto, CA 94303

Ben Yamagata
Senior Partner
Van Ness, Feldman, P.C.
1050 Thomas Jefferson
    Street, NW
Suite 700
Washington, DC 20007

Kurt E. Yeager
President
Electric Power Research
    Institute
3412 Hillview Avenue
Palo Alto, CA 94304

Michael Yokell
Director
Hagler, Bailly, Inc.
P.O. Drawer O
Boulder, CO 80306

Keiichi Yokobori
President
Asia Pacific Energy Research
    Centre
Shuwa Kamiyacho Bldg. 10F
4-3-13 Toranomon,
    Minatoku
150 Tokyo, Japan

The Aspen Institute Program on Energy, the Environment, and the Economy

The mission of **The Aspen Institute** is to enhance the quality of leadership through informed dialogue about the timeless ideas and values of the world's great cultures and traditions as they relate to the foremost challenges facing societies, organizations, and individuals. The Seminar Programs enable leaders to draw on these values to enrich their understanding of contemporary issues. The Policy Programs frame the choices that democratic societies face in terms of the enduring ideas and values derived from those traditions.

The **Program on Energy, the Environment, and the Economy** provides neutral ground for dialogue among diverse participants from the energy industry, government, environmental and other public interest groups, research institutions, the media, and elsewhere. Meetings in a non-adversarial setting encourage positive, candid interaction and seek areas of consensus or improved mutual understanding.

The **Energy Policy Forum** is now in its 21st year. Its high level participation, lively discussion, and congenial setting cause some of the most influential leaders in the energy sector to return again and again to grapple with timely topics facing energy policy makers. Session chairs and speakers serve only as discussion starters; participants with different perspectives contribute to and enrich the dialogue, with the goal of enhanced understanding and, where possible, consensus on policy recommendations.

The **Pacific Rim Series,** now in its 15th year, consists of annual workshops for experts from industry, government, and other institutions to discuss Asian energy issues.

The **Central and Eastern European Series** begun in Prague in 1995 and continued with the Krakow meeting in 1997, convenes diverse participants from the newly democratic states of the region and a few Western experts for workshops on energy problems and opportunities.

The **Series on the Environment in the 21st Century** is a continuing dialogue among business, environmental, and government leaders about developing a new, less prescriptive, and more effective environmental protection system for the United States.

Valuing Environmental Performance is a dialogue among corporations and financial institutions to find ways to better communicate the strategic value of corporate environmental behavior and for financial markets to recognize and reward improvements.

John A. Riggs is Director of The Aspen Institute's Program on Energy, the Environment, and the Economy. Prior to joining the Institute he was Deputy Assistant Secretary and Acting Assistant Secretary for Policy in the U.S. Department of Energy and staff director of the Energy and Power Subcommittee of the U.S. House of Representatives. He has also taught energy and environmental policy at the University of Pennsylvania.

Susan OMalley Wade is Senior Associate at the Program on Energy, the Environment, and the Economy. With specialties in natural resources management and planning and environmental dispute resolution, she has worked as an environmental consultant in the private sector, with the California Environmental Protection Agency, and on the staff of a U.S. House of Representatives Committee.

Appendix I
Are Oil Supply Interruptions Still Something To Worry About?

Herman Franssen
Director, Petroleum Economics Ltd.

Mr. Chairman, ladies and gentlemen:

After an absence from Aspen of about fifteen years it is good to be back here and see so many old friends and meet new ones from the energy industry, academia and the Government.

Our focus this morning is on the politics of energy; on the political context in which energy decisions are made; how this will affect where we will be in 2020 and how we will get there.

From our experience of the past quarter of a century we have learned how difficult it is to forecast the future. Whether we used sophisticated models or a simpler "bottom up" approach, we almost always missed the discontinuities which have dramatically altered the future from what we expected it to be.

A quarter of a century ago, energy analysts were concerned about the availability of conventional oil and gas resources at substantially higher prices than we have today or than we are currently projecting for the next quarter of a century. In the Seventies, energy analysts were concerned about oil "supply gaps" which needed to be filled with non-conventional fuels. None of the forecasts of the Seventies and early Eighties made reference to the exploration and production technologies which have revolutionized the upstream sector of the petroleum industry since the mid-Eighties and added significantly to global reserves and production. On the demand side, the speed of the transition away from oil to nuclear power, natural gas and coal in industry and power plants in the OECD countries again surprised most energy planners.

Neither the first nor the second oil crisis of the Seventies was foreseen but, once the 1973 crisis occurred, most analysts were convinced that prices could only go higher from then on because of assumed inelasticity of demand and non-OPEC supply. The 1986 oil price collapse and subsequent modest oil price recovery came as a big surprise to most in the oil industry.

In the 1970's, energy experts developed the so called backward-bending supply curves to show that Middle Eastern OPEC countries would limit oil production because they would not know what to do with the oil revenues if they produced beyond a certain volume. Major banks believed that the so called "low absorber" countries from the Gulf would have permanent balance of payments surpluses which, unless recycled promptly, could reduce global economic activity. In reality most oil exporting countries have suffered large budget and balance of payments deficit since the mid-Eighties when both prices and production volumes fell. Only a few have succeeded in diversifying their economies away from dependence on the oil and gas sector.

The Soviet Union was expected to become a competitor with the West for Middle Eastern oil and only modest growth in developing countries' oil demand was projected. The dissolution of the Soviet Empire in 1989 came as a big surprise as did the 1992 events in Russia which caused the collapse of communism in that country. From the late Eighties Soviet oil production collapsed as predicted in 1977, but internal demand fell as fast as supply, leaving oil exports from the Former Soviet Union to hard currency countries more or less unchanged. Russia and several of the newly independent Central Asian states offer great promise for future large scale exports to hard currency countries if and when infrastructural, political, financial and legal impediments to full development of their vast oil and gas resources have been resolved.

All of these and other events and developments in the Seventies and Eighties had a major impact on energy and oil market developments but none were predicted a quarter of a century ago.

In this session we are asked to look at energy developments in the next quarter of a century through 2020 and I hope that we will do better this time in identifying possible trends and events which may shape the future. Discontinuities, and in particular those caused by political events, will remain difficult to predict and impossible to time. The remainder of this presentation will focus on oil supply security risks.

Oil Supply Security: Is There Anything Left to Worry About?

Since 1986 oil prices have been "low" and remained mostly in the $15 to $20 trading range. The average price of Brent was just below $18 per barrel in the 1986-96 decade, compared with over $26 per barrel in the previous decade (both in dollars of the day). Despite market pressures OPEC has found it increasingly difficult to keep production discipline among its members which are all in need for revenues.

There have been no major supply interruptions causing havoc with the global economy since the second oil shock of 1979/80. The invasion of Kuwait by Iraq which led to a loss of some 3 mbd only resulted in a temporary price spike followed by a quick price collapse when it turned out that the Saudi oil fields were not in danger of being occupied. Saudi Arabia and the UAE quickly increased production by close to 4 mbd, replacing the barrels lost in the market following the Iraqi invasion.

Since the mid-Eighties Europe and the United States have become far less dependent on Middle East oil imports due to upstream developments in the Atlantic basin. Dependence on Middle eastern oil is expected to decline further by the turn of the century. Higher non-OPEC production is projected to meet more than half of incremental global demand and weakening discipline within OPEC has rendered enforcement of individual production quotas next to impossible. Instead, OPEC countries are increasingly competing not only with non-OPEC but with other OPEC countries for market share in vital strategic markets.

Subsequently market forces are expected to keep oil prices in the current $15 to $20 trading range until the sanctions on Iraq are lifted or any other major currently unforeseen changes in OPEC or non-OPEC production become apparent.

Even in the long term, it is not difficult to develop an optimistic oil price scenario for the consuming countries. While global oil demand growth is expected to remain buoyant, non-OPEC supply will also continue to increase with promising new developments in Central Asia, Russia and Latin America. OPEC is projected to expand productive capacity beyond market requirements and, once sanctions on Iraq are lifted, major expansion in that country's capacity and production is expected.

Leaving aside major supply interruptions in particular in the Middle East which from time to time could cause oil price spikes, the long term trend in oil prices is not expected to be dissimilar from the current trading range but could move from the current $15-$20 trading range to $20-$25 per barrel by the end of the next decade.Technological developments in the oil and gas industry and different perceptions within the major oil producing countries about long term opportunity cost of transportation fuels, are likely to keep the long term price below $25 per barrel in real terms. Natural gas prices, which in most markets are still linked to crude oil and product prices, may in the long term be determined by the supply and demand of natural gas itself and by other competing fuels such as coal and electricity generated by nuclear, hydro or other energy sources.

While both short and long term trends in the oil and gas industry are very positive, the geographic distribution of oil reserves is such that the world cannot move away from continued dependence on regions which are subject to potential major internal and external upheavals which from time to time can interfere with the steady flow of oil to the market.

Since the mid 1970's the OECD countries have domestic and international mechanisms to deal with supply interruptions but, current trends in the oil industry towards "just-in-time" stock management and the policies of the US and recently Germany to reduce strategic stocks for budgetary purposes could cause future problems. Just because one has not been sick for a long time is no reason to reduce one's health insurance coverage.

Potential Oil Supply Interruptions and Consequences

Last year global oil production was about 70 mbd and Middle East production and exports from the FSU (former Soviet Union) was about one-third of the total. Global spare productive capacity is estimated at around 3 mbd of which close to 2 mbd is in Saudi Arabia and 1 mbd in Kuwait and the UAE. Other producers may have surge capacity but no other known spare productive capacity. Assuming sanctions on Iraq continue through 2000, global spare capacity is unlikely to be much different from the current level by the turn of the century. This is adequate to meet a modest supply interruption. When Iraq invaded Kuwait, Saudi Arabia and the UAE increased production by almost 4 mbd and Saudi Arabia still had some 2 mbd of spare capacity left.

In case of a small supply interruption of say 2 mbd or less outside of the GCC, prices are expected to rise initially but, Saudi Arabia, Kuwait and the UAE would be able to make up for the shortfall. Moreover, coordinated action among the IEA countries and the use of oil futures are expected to mitigate the initial supply shortfall. A shortfall of this magnitude is manageable. The current practice of most refiners to keep commercial stocks low (just-in-time stock management) could, however, exacerbate upward price pressure depending on market conditions and expectations.

In the other extreme, the loss of Saudi Arabian production would imply a shortfall of 8 mbd plus two thirds of global spare capacity. Even an immediate trigger of the IEA mechanism; release of the US SPR; and full utilization of non-Saudi spare capacity would not be able to make up for much more than half of the shortfall and prices would remain high until the crisis is over.

The ability to cope with a supply shortfall will largely depend on the size of the production cut, the expected duration, the location and the speed of response of national authorities (in particular the US) and the IEA and increasingly non-IEA oil importing countries.

The ability to cope with a major supply interruption in the future has been complicated by the fact that there is far less short and medium term oil substitution ability since most oil has already been backed out of stationary uses in the industrialized countries. Moreover, sometime in the next decade about half of world oil demand will be in developing countries which are not subjected to IEA regulations in the event of a major shortfall and most of these countries do not carry 90 days of strategic and/or commercial crude oil and product stocks.

Oil Supply Interruptions: It Cannot Happen Again?

It is highly unlikely but not entirely impossible that some oil exporting countries might use oil as a weapon again as some did in 1973/74. However, more likely scenarios of supply interruptions are related to wars (such as the Iran-Iraq or Gulf wars) or internal upheavals as in Iran in 1978. While the former had a limited or relatively shortlived (or difficult to measure in the case of the Iran-Iraq war) impact on oil prices, the Iran revolution which resulted in an immediate shortfall of more than 5 mbd caused oil prices to triple by 1980.

Some analysts would argue that supply interruptions are unlikely to recur as the result of an internal upheaval in an oil producing country because whoever will take over will require oil revenues. However, destruction and chaos created by regional wars and internal upheavals, could interfere with oil production and exports. It took several years of supply interruption before Iran had returned to half of its previous capacity of more than 5 mbd and even today, a decade after the Iran-Iraq war, Iran's productive capacity is still below 4 mbd. Given the volatility of the region, it is quite possible that another supply interruption will occur in the years to come. However, the timing of major political events is impossible to predict.

Soviet experts had not foreseen the events of the late Eighties which caused the collapse of the Soviet empire and our track record predicting major upheavals elsewhere is equally poor. The US ambassador in Iran sent a cable to Washington in the summer of 1978 confirming that the Shah's regime was firmly in power in Iran and there were no signs that his regime was in immediate danger of losing control. A few months later, the Ajatola Khomeini entered Tehran and the Shah's powerful armed forces were incapable of keeping the Shah in power.

As to regional wars, many analysts said after the Gulf war in 1991 that it was unlikely that another major war would take place in the region for at least another decade. A well-known British Middle East expert wrote in June of 1989, a year before the invasion of Iraq into Kuwait:

> ...In conclusion, in military security terms, we have probably just passed a major turning point and while conflict simmers below the surface, a decade dominated by the Gulf war (Iran-Iraq war) looks as if it might be followed by a decade dominated by a Gulf peace, albeit uneasy and fragile...

Future upheavals in the Middle East can also not be excluded. The oil price collapse of 1986 had severe long term budgetary implications for a number of Middle East countries and the Gulf war (as well as purchases of new weapon systems thereafter) which was largely paid for by GCC countries further reduced the financial reserves of many countries in the region. Lower oil production since the early eighties due to OPEC policies combined with the consequences of the 1986 oil price collapse, also cut per capita income in half from the golden days of the mid-Seventies in some major Middle Eastern countries. Poor income distribution and slow progress towards participation of citizens in the government has added to internal tensions in some countries.

While budgetary constraints and slow implementation of the process of democratic participation in government are serious problems for future political stability, the real time bomb of the Nineties may prove to be rapidly growing unemployment and under employment in a number of Middle East countries. Only a small part of secondary school leavers (and even college graduates) find meaningful work in their own countries. In the past most school leavers would be absorbed in government service but budgetary restrictions have reduced government hiring. In the private sector most skilled jobs are held by foreigners and it will take time to educate sufficient local talent to take the jobs of the foreign expats. Moreover, the private sector is reluctant to replace skilled technical expats with locals because the productivity of expats tends to be higher. Unless GCC-wide labor laws are passed to cope with employment conditions of foreign technical and managerial level expats, substitution of expats by locals will be very slow.

Unskilled jobs are are almost exclusively filled by foreign labor because the social structure does not encourage local youth to compete for the jobs of the unskilled foreign workers in all sectors of the economy. Over time this may change but, for the time being most of the jobs created for local labor are in new capital-intensive petroleum or oil-related projects and the number of new openings do little to change the overall long term employment picture.

U.S. Response to Trouble in the Middle East

In 1990, the Iron Lady convinced President Bush to put together a coalition against Saddam Hussein after the invasion in Kuwait. Some Western partners reluctantly joined but the coalition held together until the end of the war. Today, the coalition has weakened because of differences in geopolitical and economic interests. France, Russia and to a lesser extent China have entered into agreements with Iraq to develop a number of very large oil fields and, together with some countries in the region, they have called for an end to the sanctions.

It is difficult to predict the nature and timing of the next conflict in the Middle East nor whether the conflict will be internal or a war involving two or more countries in the region. If the conflict is internal there may be little Western allies can do. In case of a foreign invasion, a new alliance will have to be formed which could be more difficult than it was in 1990 in view of diverging views on the Middle East between the interests of the US and its allies in the post cold war era.

Further complications in the formation of a future alliance against a would-be aggressor are related to the military costs of interventions in an era of budget constraints. In the 1990 Gulf war, Kuwait and Saudi Arabia with support from other GCC members paid for much of the immediate costs of the war. In the foreseeable future, the GCC countries will not have the vast foreign reserves they once had to pay for another Gulf war.

In the US, the Congress rallied behind the President against Iraq in part based on the fact that the US was dependent on Middle East oil and the Iraqi invasion into Kuwait threatened the major jewel in the region, Saudi Arabia. In view of new upstream developments in the Atlantic basin, the US will become less dependent on Middle East oil in the years to come than it was at the time of the Iraqi invasion into Kuwait and Europe's dependence will also not grow. By contrast, Asian nations will become increasingly dependent on the Middle East. One wonders how the Chairman of the Senate Foreign Affairs committee will react when asked to send American boys to fight in the Middle East to defend what his constituents might perceive as largely the interests of Asian oil importers. Moreover, with US dependence on Gulf oil declining, questions may be asked in this day and age of budget reviews about the estimated $30 to $60 billion the US pays for defense of the Gulf. The US Congress may increasingly wonder why other oil importers who are more dependent on the Gulf than the US, are not sharing in those costs.

The Executive branch will correctly argue that there are broader strategic interests at stake than imported oil and that it does not matter who imports oil from the region because major oil supply interruptions in the Gulf will increase global crude oil prices which will affect all economies alike. However, in the post cold war era, a more domestic policy oriented Congress may not be as easily convinced to agree to a policy of armed intervention unless there is a broad international consensus and sharing of costs.

The Middle East and Central Asia (the North Sea of the next decade) will remain troubled areas in part because of left-over disputes from the days of the Ottoman and Russian/Soviet empires.

Several of the countries in the Middle East suffer from major socio-economic problems; limited success in diversifying their economies away from the vulnerable oil and gas sector; rising populations and increasing unemployment; poor income distribution and declining acquired rights in health care and education. The region went through a short period of vast wealth accumulation between the mid-Seventies and mid-Eighties and has had difficulty adjusting to the new realities of the post-1985 era of more modest oil prices. With per capita incomes in oil export dependent countries set to decline further in the years ahead, the political stresses resulting from socio-economic problems could create further serious problems in some Middle East countries in the years ahead. Unless governments succeed in addressing these problems one can expect more tension and a potential interruption of the political *status quo*.

In light of possible socio-economic and political developments in the Middle East, it would not be prudent to assume that no serious oil supply interruption will occur in the years to come. While we have instruments to cope with supply interruptions ranging from risk management instruments of the NYMEX, IPE and private banks to implementation of IEA regulations and the use of strategic reserves of the U.S. and other IEA countries, these instruments may need to be adjusted and strengthened in the years ahead to cope with major changes in the global oil market.

Individual refiners cannot be blamed for their "just-in-time" stock management practice. They feel obliged to do so in an effort to improve margins in this poorly performing sector of the oil industry. Reduction of the strategic reserves of the U.S. and more recently Germany for budgetary reasons, if continued on a regular basis, would be shortsighted. Strategic reserves were built to protect against future major oil supply interruptions. While no one expects the deliberate use of the oil weapon in the future, accidental small to major oil supply interruptions cannot be excluded. In light of significantly reduced global oil spare capacity since the mid-Eighties and the fact that the share of oil imports by non-IEA member countries is rising rapidly, the risks related to supply interruptions would appear to be growing again. Selling off strategic oil reserves today is like reducing one's heath insurance coverage because the insured has not been sick for more than a decade.

In addition to maintaining adequate strategic reserves as an insurance against future accidental oil supply interruptions, what else can oil importing countries do to reduce risks related to oil supply interruptions?

The rising share of global oil imports by countries outside of the IEA requires closer coordination of policy between the IEA and non-member states. For this purpose the IEA has established an office which maintains liaison with governments and the private sector of non-member countries, oil importers as well as exporters. Budgetary constraints may reduce these important activities in the future. Instead of reducing non-member activities, the IEA Secretariat should be encouraged by member states to strengthen those ties and to encourage oil importing countries to maintain adequate commercial and strategic stocks as a buffer against potential future oil price shocks. Discussions with oil exporting countries have become very productive in recent years. The fact that the IEA and the GCC jointly organized a successful conference for energy experts of consuming and producing countries is a sign of changing times. Friction about the large level of oil product taxes in some oil importing countries and possible future CO_2 emission taxes are real but both oil producers and consumers agree that some form of crude oil price stability works to the advantage of both. Strategic reserves have not and will not be used to reduce normal market-induced price increases. Their prime purpose is to maintain oil supplies in the event of a major oil supply interruption. Some critics would argue that strategic reserves should be used to prevent major oil price spikes in case of a large scale supply interruption. Using the risk management mechanism of the NYMEX and the IPE could further reduce price spikes by early sell off of oil futures through the exchanges. Even producers would gain from such use of strategic reserves because a potential repetition of the events in the oil market of the Seventies could threaten an early transition away from oil in the transportation sector, the only sector left almost exclusively for the oil market.

Another area where in particular the US can make a contribution is a review of the Administration's current policy of imposing a variety of sanctions against a growing number of oil exporting countries. In addition to international sanctions against Iraq, the US has imposed sanctions against Iran, Libya and most recently Myanmar for a variety of reasons and there are ongoing discussions in the US Congress to impose sanctions against other oil producers, in particular Indonesia and Nigeria, for human rights violations.

While disagreements on human rights or other issues are understandable, imposing unilateral sanctions are not the most effective way of dealing with these issues, as the Clinton Administration has successfully argued in the case of China. Sanctions usually do not have the intended affect on the producer but instead, they tend to hurt US industries and frequently violate international agreements. Moreover, it is clear that sanctions based on human rights violations have been imposed on some countries, while others with similar records have not been touched. The US Government, which in the past strongly opposed the use of secondary boycotts when applied by the Arab League to Israel, has now adopted secondary boycotts against Iran, Libya and Cuba. Several high-level former US cabinet members and foreign policy advisors have expressed reservations against the use of secondary sanctions and have strongly argued that the President of the United States should have vetoed bills containing such provisions.

Finally, the rising number of sanctions against oil producing countries, if continued, will reduce future global spare capacity and thus could impair the long term oil supply security of the US and its allies. If sanctions against the Northern Gulf states are maintained through the end of the decade, there will be growing pressure on the GCC members to increase oil productive capacity to meet future global oil demand. There is little doubt that compliance with pressure to increase oil productive capacity while sanctions are maintained against other Middle East countries, would create further tension between the GCC and the northern Gulf states and within the GCC itself. Even if the GCC countries add additional spare capacity, recent projections by the IEA and the EIA of global demand for Middle Eastern oil by the end of the next decade suggest that major expansion of productive capacity in the Northern Gulf states will be required to meet global demand even at prices substantially above the current trading range. US sanctions against Cuba have lasted more than three decades. If Saddam Hussein would still be in power one or two decades from now and the Iranian and Libyan governments have not changed policies which have lead to US sanctions, would this imply that the US would continue to insist on maintaining sanctions against all of these countries in an increasingly oil hungry third world?

The US may have to review its current policy of dual containment against both Iraq and Iran. In a recent article in Foreign Affairs (May/June 1997), three former senior foreign policy advisors to Presidents Carter, Bush and Clinton, stated that dual containment cannot provide a sustainable basis for US policy in the Persian Gulf and that a more nuanced and differentiated approach in tune with US longer-term national interests was called for. Aware of fact that domestic political considerations guide US policy towards Iran and Iraq, they did not call for an immediate dramatic reversal in US policy but proposed consideration of "creative tradeoffs" with Iran to sustain US policy and to keep options open for the long term. The US government may want to consider working towards a consensus policy on security requirements and burden sharing with its key European and Asian allies.

Conclusion

In summary, while the medium and long term outlook for the oil market suggests ample global oil supplies to meet rising global demand initially within the current price range of $15 to $25 per barrel and at some point in the next decade possibly between $20 and $25 per barrel, the market will remain vulnerable to supply interruptions caused by wars and internal upheavals.

In the past such supply interruptions have played havoc with the global economy. OECD countries have learned a great deal from past mistakes in dealing with oil supply interruptions and monetary and fiscal policies to cope with oil price spikes. However, demand driven and policy-induced reductions in current and projected global oil productive capacity, coupled with changing global geographical oil demand patterns, could interfere with the quick implementation of global policies to cope with future oil supply interruptions.

To reduce risks associated with possible future oil supply interruptions, the IEA should be strengthened and in particular its efforts to coordinate policies with non-member countries in case of supply interruptions should be encouraged.

The US and other major OECD countries should have mechanisms in place to immediately react to supply interruptions through the use of available risk management instruments in relation to future release of strategic reserves. The past two major supply interruptions were both short-lived and their negative economic effects could have been mitigated with implementation of more enlightened government policies. The cumulative knowledge of past actions coupled with the advantage of strategic oil reserves and the availability of new instruments to cope with supply interruptions should make it easier to cope with all but the most serious supply interruption scenarios.

There is little the US and its key allies can do to influence internal developments in the Middle East. The US may, however, consider reviewing its current policy of dual containment in order to reduce long term pressures on the GCC and to encourage future surplus oil productive capacity needed to maintain price stability which in the long term serves producers and consumers alike. In the meantime, improved national and international preparedness to cope with major possible oil supply interruptions, would appear to be the best insurance against a repetition of the oil price triggered economic recessions of the Seventies and early Eighties.

Appendix II
Politics, Power, and Petroleum

Robin West
Chairman, The Petroleum Finance Company

Politics, Power & Petroleum

Robin West

Chairman, The Petroleum Finance Company, Ltd.

Presentation to the

Aspen Institute

Aspen

July 6, 1997

FIGURE 1

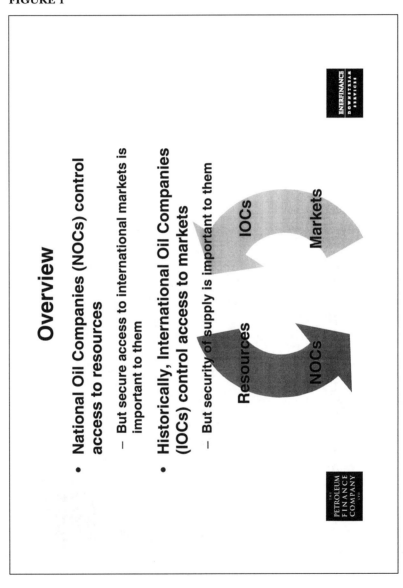

FIGURE 2

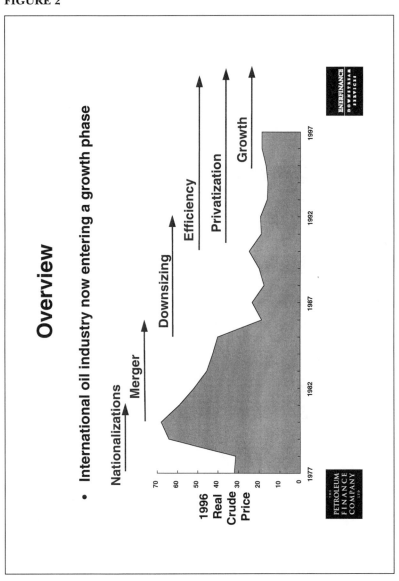

FIGURE 3

FIGURE 4

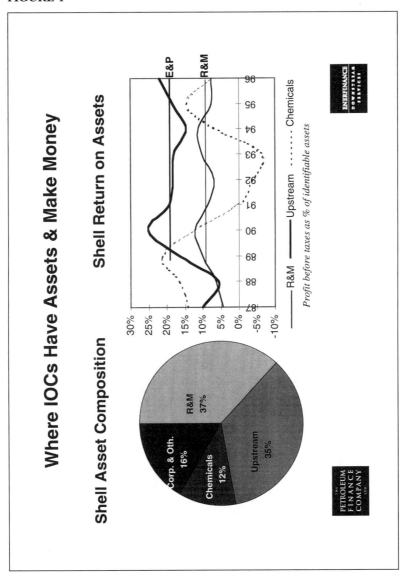

FIGURE 5

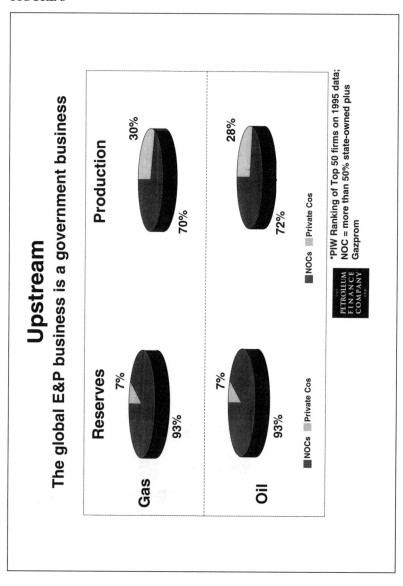

FIGURE 6

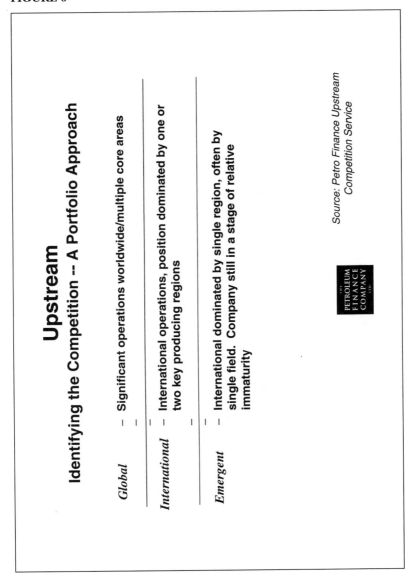

Upstream
Identifying the Competition -- A Portfolio Approach

Global — Significant operations worldwide/multiple core areas

International — International operations, position dominated by one or two key producing regions

Emergent — International dominated by single region, often by single field. Company still in a stage of relative immaturity

Source: Petro Finance Upstream Competition Service

FIGURE 7

Upstream -- Core Areas

- Core Areas -- Where firms make most profits
- Definition:
  - Reserves material to the company's asset base
  - Several giant discoveries but numerous smaller fields contribute economies of scale over time
  - Repeatable investment opportunities in the area
  - Typically large license areas "locked-up"
  - Company does not always originate the exploration play (BHP/Bass Strait; ARCO/NW Java; Chevron/Angola)

FIGURE 8

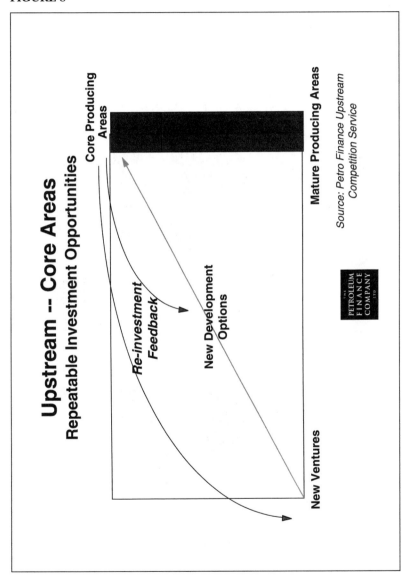

FIGURE 9

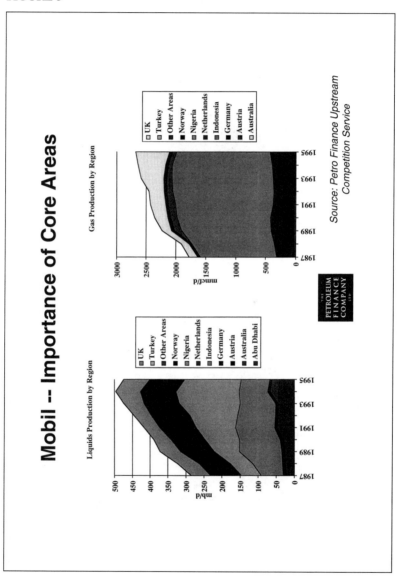

FIGURE 10

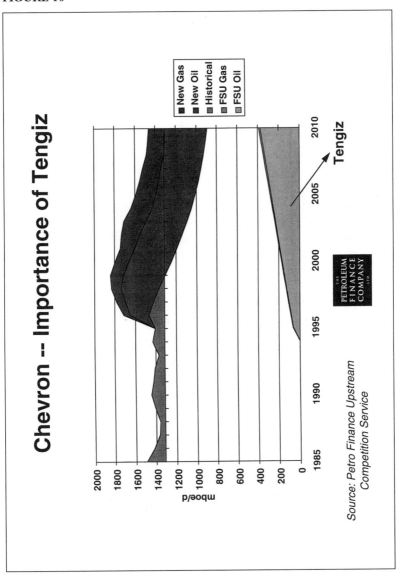

FIGURE 11

Risk Differentiation

Above Ground Risks

domestic political attitudes toward foreign oil companies
labor union issues
environmental sensitivities
civil strife
transportation routes - boundary issues
instability of joint venture contracts exposure to taxation

Below Ground Risks

exploration risks
reservoir performance
downward revisions in reserves
difficult drilling conditions downhole

Source: Petro Finance Upstream Competition Service

THE PETROLEUM FINANCE COMPANY LTD.

FIGURE 12

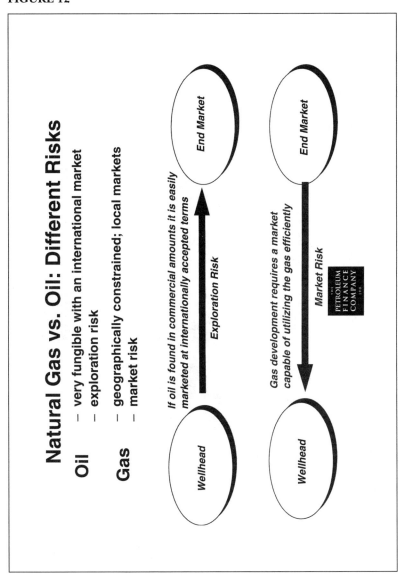

FIGURE 13

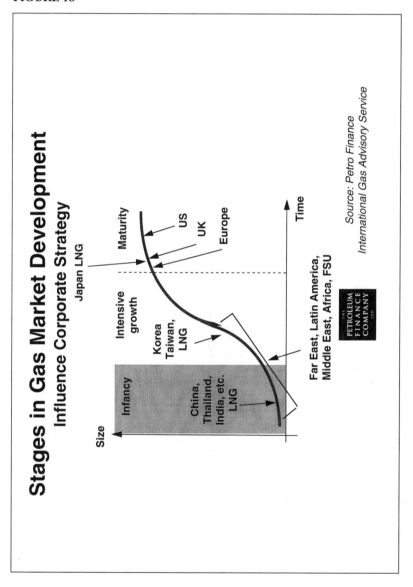

FIGURE 14

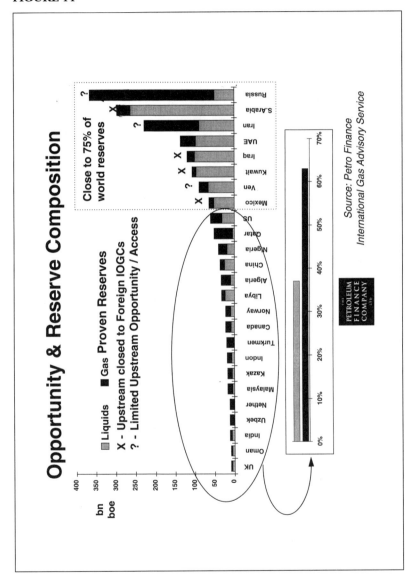

Appendix III
Atmospheric Stabilization and The Role of Energy Technology

Jae Edmonds, James Dooley, Marshall Wise

A version of this paper was published as Edmonds, JA, Dooley, JJ, Wise, MA "Atmospheric Stabilization: The Role of Energy Technology," in Climate Change Policy, Risk Prioritization, and US Economic Growth, June, 1997.

Abstract

Stabilization of the concentration of greenhouse gases in the atmosphere as per the Framework Convention on Climate Change (FCCC) is a non-trivial goal. Attaining this goal implies that global fossil fuel carbon emissions must eventually be phased out. The urgency of the phase out depends on the desired steady-state concentration of gases such as CO_2. At present the goal of atmospheric stabilization is aspirational. National goals have not been spelled out. There are no enforcement mechanisms or penalties. If the goal of atmospheric stabilization is to make the transition from aspiration to reality, the degree to which it is in conflict with other goals such as health, safety, and growth of material income must be minimized.

The costs of stabilizing the atmosphere depend on the timing with which emissions mitigation occurs, the flexibility available to participating nations in mitigating emissions, and the available technologies. Stabilizing the atmosphere with the present suite, 1990 vintage, of technologies could cost more than $10 trillion if 550 ppmv were the desired goal, even with the most efficient implementation over space and time. Stabilizing the atmosphere with the suite of technologies anticipated in the IPCC IS92a scenario significantly could lower the cost by an order of magnitude if a set of institutions can be developed to provide flexibility in when and where emissions reductions occur. But the institutional arrangements needed are potentially unprecedented. They require the creation of mechanisms as effective as tradable emissions permits. The use of tradable emissions permits themselves would require negotiating their allocation and the creation of enforcement mechanisms. The negotiation of "fair" economic burdens among the participants could be a time consuming process, especially if it extends beyond Annex I countries, as it inevitably must.

The development of advanced non-carbon energy technologies holds the promise of reducing the costs of atmospheric stabilization. While advanced technology does offer promise, its development is uncertain and the costs of reaching the levels assumed in this paper could be substantial. If the technologies assumed here do not come along as predicted in this study, then the costs of stabilization will be very substantial. The successful development and deployment of such technologies could eliminate the need for enforcement. The stabilization path would be enforced by the market. Firms using inefficient, high-emissions technologies would no longer be competitive. A variety of technologies both near at hand and in their embryonic stage exist which could minimize the burden of transition to low and non-carbon emitting energy systems. Their rates of development and deployment will be affected by the level of United States energy R&D investment. As R&D is the classic example of underproduction due to market failure, increasing R&D easily falls within the realm of a "no regrets" action. Unfortunately, at present, United States energy R&D expenditure levels have been falling, and there is no good reason to believe that the trend will soon reverse on its own.

Disclaimer

While we are grateful for the financial support for the conduct of our research provided by the Electric Power Research Institute (EPRI) and the United States Department of Energy (DOE), the views expressed in this paper are solely those of the authors and were formed and expressed without reference to positions taken by these institutions. The views of the authors are not intended to either reflect or imply positions of either EPRI or DOE.

Acknowledgments

We would like to express our appreciation to the Electric Power Research Institute (EPRI) and to the United States Department of Energy (DOE) for their support. This work was supported in part by the EPRI under contract number DE-AC06-76RLO1831 the DOE under contract number DE-AC06-76RLO1830. Special thanks to Richard Richels for providing many useful comments during the conduct of this research. Many thanks to John Clarke, Chester Cooper, John Houghton, and Margo Thorning for comments on an earlier draft.

Introduction

The Framework Convention on Climate Change (FCCC; United Nations, 1992), signed by 155 nations as of April 1996, seeks to stabilize the concentration of greenhouse gases in the atmosphere. This goal is not further defined, however, leaving open several questions including the level at which to seek a stable concentration, and the time frame in which to accomplish the goal.

Considerable research has been undertaken considering the goal's implications for human activities. The IPCC (1995) undertook calculations which prescribed a set of anthropogenic carbon emissions paths leading to stabile CO_2 concentrations at levels ranging from 350 parts per million volume (ppmv) to 750 ppmv. In 1994 the concentration of CO_2 in the atmosphere was 354 ppmv. Thus the scenarios spanned a range of concentrations which are lower than present to more than double the pre-industrial concentration of 275 ppmv.

There are in principle an infinite number of anthropogenic CO_2 emissions trajectories which can be followed which are consistent with any arbitrary ceiling. Each of the emissions paths has a variety of accompanying implications. Wigley, Richels and Edmonds (WRE,1996) argued that trajectories, which have greater near-term emissions, relative to IPCC (1995), have lower near-term economic costs and higher cumulative emissions, but higher near-term temperatures.[1] For con-

**FIGURE 1: TWO SETS OF ANTHROPOGENIC CARBON
EMISSIONS TRAJECTORIES CONSISTENT WITH VARIOUS
LONG-TERM STEADY-STATE CO$_2$ CONCENTRATIONS—S SERIES
AND WRE SERIES**

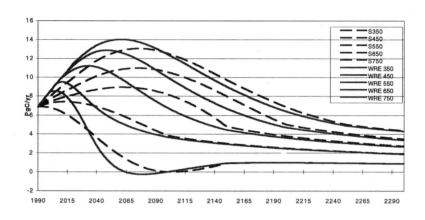

centration ceilings of 450 ppmv or higher, emissions reductions would not be required until after the year 2000. This sparked a controversy. Papers such as Grubb (1996a,b), Grubb, et al. (1995), Chapuis, et al. (1996), and Ha-Duong, et al. (1996) argued that the delay in emissions mitigation was undesirable, but the quantitative differences between WRE and others have diminished such that in Ha-Duong, et al. (1996) the quantitative results are virtually identical to WRE for commonly prescribed steady-state CO$_2$ concentrations, even though the economic models vary substantially. Nevertheless, the "right ceiling," or optimal steady-state concentration to choose, remains a matter of debate.

The purpose of this paper is to generate information that could be useful to the negotiation process by exploring some of the implications of alternative CO$_2$ concentration ceilings for a dynamic portfolio of policy responses. We are particularly interested in the role of technology in determining the eventual cost of achieving various steady-state concentration objectives. A wide array of technologies with the potential to dramatically lower the cost of achieving steady-state CO$_2$ concentrations have been identified for both the near-term (10-20 years) as well as the mid-term (20-50 years). It is well known that R&D plays a critical role in shaping future technologies, though the mechanisms by which the rate and scope of R&D influences technological progress remain poorly understood (DOE,1996). It is clear that both public and private energy-related R&D in the United States, and particularly non-fossil fuel related energy-related R&D, has been declining over the past decade. This is a trend which does not bode well for the realization of low-cost stabilization of the atmosphere.

The "Right" Ceiling

Analysis would be much easier if the determination of the steady-state atmospheric CO_2 concentration were defined. But there is presently no consensus regarding the optimal or "right" concentration at which to stabilize atmospheric CO_2. The FCCC provides no specific guidance, and research results vary. Traditional cost-benefit analysis seems to indicate that optimal concentration might be rather high, above 600 ppmv (Nordhaus, 1994; Peck and Teisberg, 1995: Manne, Mendelsohn and Richels, 1993; Kolstad, 1993). But the analysis of costs and benefits is limited by the highly aggregated and stylized treatment of damages (IPCC, 1996c), which in turn reflect the vague relationship between emissions, climate change, and climate-change damage currently embodied in all cost-benefit models. Thus, Cline (1992) has argued that relatively stringent optimal emissions controls could be consistent with the cost-benefit framing of the problem.

Incorporating uncertainty into the analytical framework does not appear to significantly change the results. Manne and Richels (1993), Kolstad (1994) and Dowlatabadi (1996) have shown that optimal emissions mitigation trajectories for pre-scribed steady-state CO_2 concentrations are largely unchanged by the inclusion of uncertainty. Dowlatabadi (1996) finds that if the desired steady-state ceiling is near at hand that uncertainty in the mitigation response to policy signals could imply greater near-term emissions mitigation efforts than under a deterministic case. But Manne and Richels (1993) found that uncertainty in the target led to little near-term emissions mitigation. Ha-Duong, et al. (1996) examined a case similar to Manne and Richels (1993) except that they delayed the date at which uncertainty in determining the "right" concentration ceiling was resolved. This delay led their model to select an emissions path consistent with the lowest "possible" ceiling. But the Ha-Duong, et al. result appears to be more an artifact of the particular methodology employed for the analysis than a robust finding.[2]

The Three Phases of Stabilization Trajectories

While the optimal concentration at which to stabilize the concentration of atmospheric CO_2 remains undetermined, several observations seem to transcend this uncertainty. For all concentration levels 450 ppmv and higher, all of the emissions trajectories exhibit three distinct phases. The first phase is characterized by increasing global emissions. The second phase is one in which emissions peak and are relatively stable. And the third phase is one in which emissions decline in perpetuity. If a steady-state CO_2 concentration target less than 450 ppmv is chosen only the third, emissions reduction phase, is relevant. For example, to affect the S350 case, emissions should have peaked in 1994 and be declining. For the WRE350 case global emissions do not peak until the year 2005, but they must decline perpetually thereafter, and for a period become negative.

The general nature of the three phases yields some important insights. First, any policy prescription which begins with the proposition that global CO_2 emissions must decline relative to 1990 levels beginning immediately implies a concentration below 500 ppmv until the end of the next century. However, unless further measures are taken to insure a long-term decline in emissions, the program will not produce a steady-state atmospheric concentration.

Timing of the three phases differs somewhat between the S series and WRE series. Table 1 shows the date at which emissions begin to depart from the reference, IS92a, scenario, the date at which emissions reach their maximum, and the maximum value they attain.

We arbitrarily define the deflection date to be the year in which emissions in the IS92a trajectory first exceed emissions in the stabilization trajectory by more than 0.1 PgC/yr. In the S series of stabilization trajectories emissions depart immediately from the reference trajectory, while in the WRE cases the deflection date is postponed. Global emissions should have begun to depart from the IS92a scenario no later than the year 1992 to satisfy even the least stringent S series atmospheric stabilization emissions trajectory. The degree of postponement in the WRE trajectories relative to the S series depends on the eventual steady-state level. In no WRE case is deflection delayed beyond the year 2023 and for the 450 ppmv steady-state level deflection occurs in the year 2007.

The date at which emissions reach their maximum is systematically later in the S series of trajectories than in the corresponding WRE series. Thus, the WRE cases require long-term global emissions declines to begin earlier than in the S series cases. For the 450 ppmv steady-state the maximum is attained in 2011 for the WRE and in 2013 in the S series, though the S series requires far greater near-term emissions controls, with maximum global emissions reaching only 7.4 PgC/yr in that year. The 550 ppmv steady-state peak emissions is also approximately 2 PgC/yr lower in the S series than in the WRE series, with peak emissions occurring 30 years earlier in the WRE trajectory. The greatest difference between WRE and the S series occurs in the 550 ppmv steady-state. In this case emissions peak in the year 2033 for WRE and then begin their long term decline from a maximum global emission rate of 11.2 PgC/yr. This contrasts with the year 2063 peak emission of 8.9 PgC/yr in the S series.

TABLE 1: TIMING OF EMISSIONS MITIGATION UNDER WRE AND S TRAJECTORIES

Steady-State Concentration	WRE			S		
	Deflection Date a	Maximum Date	Maximum Emission b	Deflection Date a	Maximum Date	Maximum Emission b
350 ppmv	2001	2005	8.5	1991	1994	6.9
450 ppmv	2007	2011	9.5	1991	2013	7.4
550 ppmv	2013	2033	11.2	1991	2063	8.9
650 ppmv	2018	2049	12.9	1992	2075	11.0
750 ppmv	2023	2062	14.0	1992	2076	13.1

[a]The deflection date is the year in which emissions in the IS92a trajectory first exceed emissions in the stabilization trajectory by more than 0.1 PgC/yr.

[b]PgC/yr total carbon emissions including emissions from land-use change and cement manufacture.

Participation

The foregoing discussion reflects a global perspective. But the FCCC and the Conference of the Parties (COP, 1995) differentiates responsibilities associated with Annex I3 and non-Annex I nations in emissions mitigation. Annex I nations are to take the first steps. It is abundantly clear that Annex I nations cannot provide sufficient emissions reductions to affect any steady-state concentration 750 ppmv or lower.

Figure 2 shows Annex I emissions trajectories consistent with WRE and S series emissions trajectories on the assumption that non-Annex I nations emissions are unaffected by Annex I reductions. As Edmonds et al. (1995) and Richels et al. (1996) have shown, non-participating nations may have unintended changes in emissions through trade effects. Even zero Annex I emissions are ultimately insufficient to affect either the WRE or the S trajectories. Eventually, non-Annex I emissions exceed the WRE and S trajectories.

We can also consider the issue from another perspective. We construct a simple hypothetical Annex I obligation for the purposes of exploring the implications for non-Annex I nations.

**FIGURE 2: ANNEX I EMISSIONS TRAJECTORIES NECESSARY TO
AFFECT WRE AND S ATMOSPHERIC STABILIZATION SCENARIOS
ON THE ASSUMPTION THAT NON-ANNEX I EMISSIONS ARE
UNAFFECTED.**

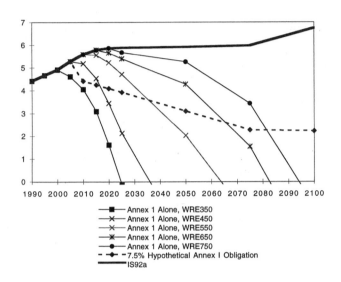

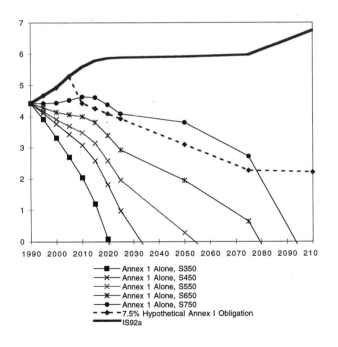

FIGURE 3: NON-ANNEX I EMISSIONS TRAJECTORIES NECESSARY TO AFFECT WRE AND S ATMOSPHERIC STABILIZATION SCENARIOS ON THE ASSUMPTION THAT ANNEX I EMISSIONS ARE REDUCED AS PER HYPOTHETICAL ACTION PROFILE.

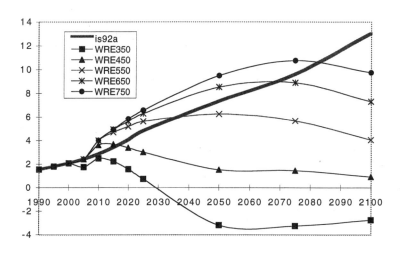

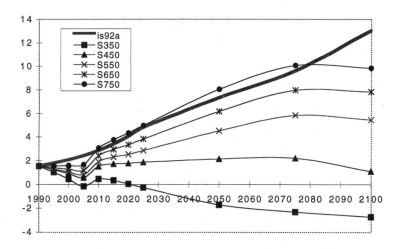

We assume that Annex I nations return emissions to 1990 levels in the year 2000 and hold them at that level until the year 2005 at which time emissions begin to decline, relative to 1990 levels, 0.75%/yr until they reach 50% of 1990 emissions at which point they are maintained constant for the remainder of the century. This hypothetical Annex I obligation has not been proposed by any government, but is consistent in its general outline with proposals that have been put forward.

We have examined Annex I emissions to satisfy atmospheric stabilization objectives on the assumption that non-Annex I nations do not participate. We can also compute the required non-Annex I emissions required to achieve atmospheric stabilization objectives on the assumption that Annex I takes specific actions such as those outlined above. Required non-Annex I emissions are displayed in Figure 3.

Non-Annex I emissions under WRE and S series trajectories are very different. Under the S series, non-Annex I emissions must be reduced simultaneously with Annex I emissions to affect any trajectory other than S750. Emissions reduction requirements vary with time, see Table 2. For comparison purposes Table 2 reports hypothetical Annex I emissions reductions relative to the IS92a trajectory. The S series, non-Annex I emissions reductions are a larger fraction of IS92a emissions than is the case for Annex I for S350, S450 and S550.[4]

Under the WRE trajectory non-Annex I nations have excess inventories which, depending on the terms of agreement, could potentially be either banked for future use or sold to Annex I nations. The value of these emissions rights would vary with time depending on the marginal cost of emissions mitigation. As a finite financial asset, their value would be expected to rise at the rate of interest.[5]

TABLE 2: NON-ANNEX I EMISSIONS REDUCTION REQUIREMENTS AS A PERCENTAGE OF IS92A LEVELS NECESSARY TO AFFECT S SERIES ATMOSPHERIC STABILIZATION TRAJECTORIES WHERE ANNEX I NATIONS UNDERTAKE PRESCRIBED EMISSIONS REDUCTIONS

Year	S350	S450	S550	S650	S750	Annex I*
1995	28%	17%	14%	8%	0%	5%
2000	53%	32%	25%	14%	-1%	10%
2005	71%	41%	30%	15%	-4%	16%
2010	77%	41%	27%	9%	-14%	24%
2015	84%	44%	27%	8%	-16%	29%
2020	94%	52%	33%	13%	-12%	33%
2025	101%	58%	37%	17%	-7%	36%
2050	121%	68%	36%	13%	-12%	51%
2075	123%	76%	38%	16%	-5%	63%
2100	121%	92%	58%	40%	25%	67%

* By assumption Annex I nations return emissions to 1990 levels in the year 2000 and hold them at that level until the year 2005 at which time emissions begin to decline, relative to 1990 levels, 0.75%/yr until the reach 50% of 1990 emissions at which point they are maintained constant for the remainder of the century.

Cost, Timing, Technology, and Flexibility

We estimate the cost of stabilizing the atmosphere using the MiniCAM 2.0 model (Edmonds, Wise, Pitcher, Richels, Wigley, and MacCracken, 1996; Barns, et al. 1992; Edmonds, Reilly, Gardner, and Brenkert, 1986; and Edmonds and Reilly, 1995). Costs are estimated for three sets of cases: WRE, S, and Optimal steady-state concentration trajectories. The optimal steady-state concentration trajectory is the least cost emissions path consistent with cumulative emissions given by WRE.[6] Costs are computed in the year incurred and discounted to the present at 5%/yr. Results are displayed in Figure 4 in 1990 US dollars.

For any set of trajectories, S, WRE or Optimal, costs decline as the steady-state concentration rises. The decline in costs between 450 ppmv and 550 ppmv is rapid particularly for the Optimal and WRE cases. For any concentration level, costs for

FIGURE 4: MiniCAM 2.0 COSTS OF STABILIZE THE ATMOSPHERE CO$_2$ CONCENTRATION AT LEVELS RANGING FROM 450PPMV TO 750 PPMV FOR THREE ALTERNATIVE SETS OF EMISSIONS TRAJECTORIES (S, WRE, AND OPTIMAL) AND ONE NON-STABILIZATION CASE.

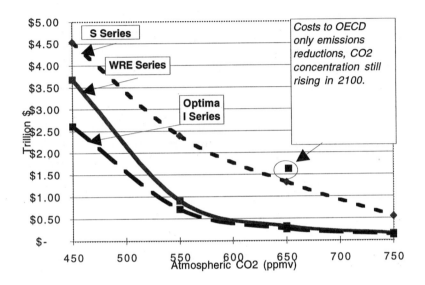

the Optimal case are always lowest followed by the WRE and S cases. The reduction in costs between the WRE and S series cases ranges from about 23% for the 450 ppmv case to more than 300% for the 650 ppmv case. Further cost reductions in moving from the WRE to the Optimal case are generally in the neighborhood of 25% except for the 450 ppmv case where reductions reach 40%.

Richels and Edmonds (1994) have shown that the cost of efficiently stabilizing the atmosphere at 500 ppmv may be only half the cost of efficiently stabilizing emissions. The cost of stabilizing the atmosphere at 450 ppmv amounts to approximately 0.5% of global GDP, and the cost of stabilizing at 550 ppmv is only 0.1% of global GDP. Costs are the direct consequence of three critical assumptions. First, emissions reduction are carried on according to the WRE trajectory. Second, substantial technological change occurs over the course of the next century. And third, emissions reductions are undertaken wherever they are cheapest. Failure of any of these assumption implies substantially different, and higher costs.

We have explored some of the cost implications of non-optimal emissions mitigation trajectories. There are penalties associated with inflexibility in the implementation of emissions abatement. Consider the case where only OECD nations undertake emissions reductions, stabilizing their individual emissions at 1990 levels until the year 2010, at which time emissions are reduced to 20% of 1990 levels and held there indefinitely, and that emissions reductions must be undertaken in the responsible region without intertemporal emissions shifting. The effect of these emissions reductions is to reduce the year 2100 concentration by 53 ppmv. OECD only reductions are insufficient to stabilize the atmosphere. Both global emissions and concentrations of CO_2 are rising in the year 2100. This reduction occurs at a present discounted cost of \$1.6 trillion over the period 1990 through 2050. The concentration and cost are shown on Figure 4 for comparison.

Because concentrations are rising in the year 2100 in the OECD only case, it is impossible to provide a true comparison with the S, WRE, and optimal cases, all of which are associated with steady-state concentrations. Nevertheless, costs in the OECD only case are of a magnitude similar to those expended to achieve a steady-state of 500 ppmv in the optimal case. Even employing the S series, inefficient emission time-path yields a true steady-state concentration less than the year 2100 concentration.

Technology also plays a critical role in determining costs. Costs associated with the S and WRE emissions trajectories assume rather substantial technological progress continues throughout the remainder of the century. For example the efficiency of the average fossil fuel powerplant is assumed increase at more than 1.0%/yr between 1990 and 2050, from 0.33 to 0.66. Exogenous end-use energy intensity proceeds at between 0.5%/yr (OECD nations) and 2.5%/yr (Eastern Europe and the Former Soviet Union). The cost of non-fossil fuel electric power generating technologies, other than nuclear and hydroelectric, declines at an average annual rate of 4.5%/yr between 1990 and 2025, and at 1.25%/yr from 2025 to the year 2100. And the cost of biomass energy production declines at an annual rate of one percent per year between 1990 and 2100 from 1990 values ranging from $2.50/GJ to $4.40/GJ, depending on the location and scale of production. Furthermore, labor productivity increases the rate of economic growth at an average annual rate of 2.3%/yr between 1990 and 2100. All of this reduces energy intensity over the period 1990 to 2100 at an average annual rate of 1.0%/yr, making it less costly to satisfy emissions reduction objectives. These energy technology developments are specified exogenously. They come at no additional cost to society and are sometimes referred to as the "free lunch." These technologies penetrate the market on the basis of their relative attractiveness.

To explore the role of energy technology we have constructed two cases in which we stabilize the atmosphere with technologies other than those assumed to be available in IS92a. In the first case energy technology is assumed to be static at 1990 costs and efficiency rates. In the second case we explore the benefits to be obtained by assuming that cost and performance of technologies identified in IPCC (1996b) materialize by the year 2020. The resulting present discounted cost of realizing alternative steady-state concentrations with associated WRE emissions trajectories are shown in Table 3 as a percentage of present discounted GDP. For contrast we also report results for the IS92a technology assumptions.

The advanced technology case examines technologies which might be introduced in the future, but which are not presently available. These technologies include: advanced liquefied hydrogen fuel cells; hydrogen transformation from natural gas, biomass, or electrolysis; non-fossil fuel electric power generating technologies including solar photovoltaic, nuclear fusion, and wind, and commercial biomass energy production. Mean potential costs for the non-carbon electric technology set is

FIGURE 5: REFERENCE CASE WITH ADVANCED ENERGY TECHNOLOGIES COMPARED TO VARIOUS WRE EMISSIONS PATHS.

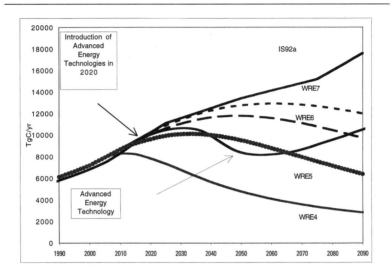

assumed to decline to a cost of \$0.04/kWh by 2020 and decline 0.5%/yr thereafter. Biomass energy is assumed to be available at costs ranging from the \$1.40/GJ to \$2.40/GJ. The impact of these technologies on the cost of stabilizing atmospheric CO_2 concentrations at various levels is reported in Table 3. For the 450 ppmv steady-state the present discounted value is approximately three trillion 1990 US dollars, and for the 550 ppmv steady-state the present discounted value is approximately one trillion 1990 US dollars. The value of these technologies declines precipitously as the steady-state CO_2 concentration rises above 550 ppmv.

Stabilizing the concentration of atmospheric CO_2 is potentially achievable at levels of present discounted costs below one percent of global GDP. Realizing this potential requires substantial improvement in energy technologies relative to 1990, and institutional mechanisms for reducing emissions whenever and wherever in the world it is cheapest. Failure to provide either the technology or institutions can lead to ineffective and expensive emissions mitigation.

TABLE 3: PRESENT DISCOUNTED COST TO STABILIZE ATMOSPHERIC CO2 CONCENTRATIONS AT ALTERNATIVE LEVELS AS PERCENT OF GDP A

Ceiling (ppmv)	IS92a Technology	Static Technology	Advanced Technology
450	0.47%	2.73%	0.05%
550	0.12%	1.60%	0.00%
650	0.04%	1.20%	0.00%
750	0.02%	1.03%	0.00%

[a]Both costs and GDP are discounted at 5% and summed.

One of the attractive features of technology development is that in a market economy, there is little or no need for further institutional arrangements. If the non-carbon energy technologies are made sufficiently efficient and cost competitive, stabilization occurs in the reference case. Costs of stabilization go to zero for higher steady-state concentrations, because under non-climate-policy intervention scenarios, emissions are below the WRE emissions trajectories until far into the next century, Figure 5. Enforcement costs go to zero as firms which fail to reduce emissions are driven out of business by competition. Furthermore, where successful, the new technology becomes the basis of comparative advantage and national export.

An Energy Revolution Waiting in the Wings?

In the foregoing analysis of the cost of stabilizing the atmospheric concentration of CO_2, we not only assumed that non-carbon technologies identified in IPCC (1996b) became available in the year 2020, but that the class of non-carbon energy technologies continued to improve over time. This expectation is based on two foundations. First, the assumption is consistent with historical experience. New technologies have continually emerged over time. And, second, there are a variety of scientific developments, which though at an early stage, could revolutionize the production and use of energy.

One class of technologies currently being developed seeks to combine recent advances nanotechnology— the ability to design and build structures atom-by-atom—with an emerging class of microtechnologies—using channels on the order of a few hundred microns to more finely control traditional chemical and energy processes. Nano[7]-structure versions of key energy components such as highly selective membranes combined with the heat and mass transfer benefits of microtechnologies offer the potential for substantial improvements in energy transformation and ultimately in CO_2 emission reductions. This approach offers many substantial benefits, including for example, improved heat and mass transfer[8], improved control of chemical reaction rates[9], improved mobility[10], greater safety and reliability[11], and higher power densities (Wegeng et al., 1996).

Technologies first developed for the manufacture of microprocessors in computers can potentially be applied to energy

FIGURE 6: U.S. INVESTMENT IN ENERGY R&D

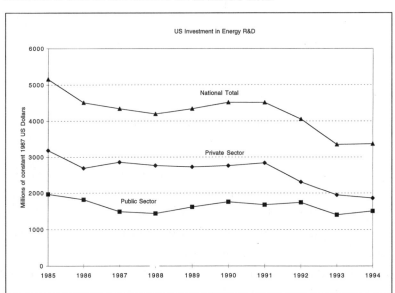

**FIGURE 7: PUBLIC AND PRIVATE ENERGY R&D PORTFOLIOS
1985–1994, FUNDING FOR ENERGY R&D BY PRIMARY FUEL TYPE**

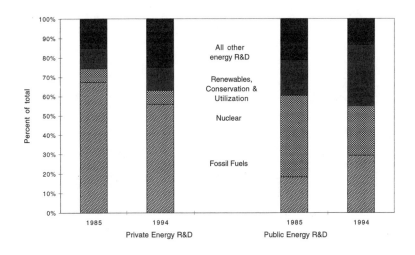

systems. The technology platform for a number of chemical and energy applications—microchannel heat exchangers, gas absorbers, liquid-liquid extractors, reactors, and microactuators for pumps, valves and compressors—are all being developed. These individual components can be linked in parallel and series arrangements on sheets with up to 103 individual components, creating the potential for a variety of advanced energy product applications. Some of the most promising technologies at present are related to fuel cells and heat pumps. Fuel cell applications include high efficiency vehicle applications, and distributed utility fuel cells, while the microscale absorption cycle heat pumps may be used for vehicular and distributed space conditioning applications.

While it is difficult to see precisely which applications will proved to be important in shaping energy futures, it is clear that energy systems of the future are potentially vastly different and more efficient from those presently available.

FIGURE 8: FEDERAL SUPPORT FOR ENERGY R&D 1985–1994

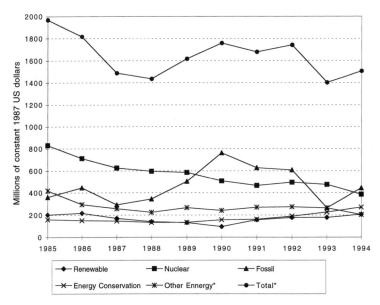

The Scale of R&D

While technology appears to hold the promise of low cost atmospheric stabilization, recent energy R&D investment levels in the United States have been declining. Measured in almost any way United States investment in energy research and development (R&D) has declined substantially over the last decade. For example, total (public and private) United States expenditures for energy R&D declined from $4.9 billion in 1985 to $4.2 billion in 1994, a real decline of 42%—or expressed in constant 1987 US dollars the numbers are $5.2 billion in 1985 and only $3.4 billion in 1994 (Dooley 1996). Furthermore as a percent of GDP, United States investments in energy R&D have declined from 0.074% of GPD in 1985 to 0.035% of GDP in 1994 (Dooley 1996).

Over the period 1985-1994, the private sector in the United States funded between 50-60% of the national energy R&D

effort. Figure 6 presents data on total United States (public and private) investments in energy R&D in constant 1987 United States dollars. The composition of the public and private sector portfolios for 1985 and 1994 are displayed in Figure 7. Fossil energy R&D is the dominant form of private sector R&D. Private-sector investments in fossil energy R&D declined from 67 to 56% of total private-sector energy R&D from 1985 to 1994. Much of this decline is attributable to sizable (24% in real terms) cuts in energy R&D funding at the 25 largest United States energy (mainly oil and gas) producing firms (Dooley 1996).

In contrast, federal funding for fossil energy R&D has dramatically increased its share of total federal energy R&D, largely due to the Department of Energy's Clean Coal Technology Demonstration Program. Fossil energy R&D increased from 16% of all federal energy R&D investments in 1985 to 29% of the total in 1994.

Nuclear energy R&D made up a substantially smaller percentage of the public's energy R&D portfolio and remained a minor component of the private sector's energy R&D portfolio over the period 1985-1994. For the federal government, nuclear energy R&D went from 43% of its total energy R&D budget in 1985 to 26% in 1994. In the private sector, nuclear energy R&D remained at about 7% of its total energy R&D effort throughout this period.

Both the public and the private sectors have increased the percentages of their energy R&D portfolios that are directed towards energy efficiency, renewable energy, and energy utilization R&D. Energy R&D in this area has increased from 18% to 32% of all federal energy R&D from 1985-1994, while the private-sector's investments in this area have increased slightly from 10-12%. However, it is important to note that for reasons discussed elsewhere (Dooley 1996), data presented here for private sector energy efficiency, renewable energy, and energy utilization R&D most likely understate industry's true investment levels in this area; therefore, it is likely that energy efficiency, renewable energy, and energy utilization R&D accounts for more than 12% of industry's current energy R&D portfolio.

There is no reason to believe that United States energy R&D investment levels will rise soon. Teich (1996) estimates that pressure to reduce the federal deficit will result in further reductions of between 19 and 23% in real federal R&D spending by the year 2002. In the private sector restructuring and deregulation of the natural gas and electric utility industries has caused firms to focus on short-term cost cutting measures such as reductions in energy R&D investments. For example, since the Gas Research Institute's R&D funding peaked in 1992 at $212 million it has declined to $175 million in 1996, a real decline of 26%. The Electric Power Research Institute R&D funding declined from its peak of $509 million in 1993 to $441 million in 1996, a real decline of 20% (Dooley 1996).

There is some evidence that regulation can induce R&D and stimulate technological change. The example of phaseout of chlorofluorocarbons (CFCs) is often cited. Here the prospect of regulation of these substances led firms to examine alternatives that had not previously been considered. That research led to the conclusion that the cost of regulation was lower than had been previously estimated. The innovating firms then stood to benefit from the imposition of new regulations which would create a market for the non-CFC technology. Opposition faded and the substances were indeed regulated.

Other cases exist in which regulation was unsuccessful in inducing successful technological change. The example of the State of California's regulation of transportation emissions is a case in point. Here stringent regulations on emissions were anticipated to lead to the development of technology capable of racially reducing emissions. This has not occurred.

It is certainly possible that the imposition of stringent constraints on energy-related carbon emissions would lead to the redirection of resources toward energy R&D and induce sweeping technological improvements. But the evidence for such linkages is limited.

Conclusions

Stabilization of the concentration of greenhouse gases in the atmosphere as per the Framework Convention on Climate Change (FCCC) is a non-trivial goal. Attaining this goal implies that global fossil fuel carbon emissions must eventually be phased out. The urgency with which the phase out depends on the desired steady-state concentration of gases such as CO_2.

At present the goal of atmospheric stabilization is aspirational. National goals have not been spelled out. There are no enforcement mechanisms or penalties. If the goal of atmospheric stabilization is to make the transition from aspiration to reality, the degree to which it is in conflict with other goals such as health, safety, and growth of material income must be minimized.

The costs of stabilizing the atmosphere depend on the timing with which emissions mitigation occurs, the flexibility available to participating nations in mitigating emissions, and the available technologies. Stabilizing the atmosphere with the present suite, 1990 vintage, of technologies would cost between one and three percent of present discounted GDP even with the most efficient implementation over space and time. Stabilizing the atmosphere with the suite of technologies anticipated in the IPCC IS92a scenario significantly lowers costs if a set of institutions can be developed to provide flexibility in when and where emissions reductions occur.

But the institutional arrangements needed are potentially unprecedented. They require the creation of mechanisms as effective as tradable emissions permits. The use of tradable emissions permits themselves would require negotiating their allocation and the creation of enforcement mechanisms. The negotiation of "fair" economic burdens among the participants could be a time consuming process, especially if it extends beyond Annex I countries, as it inevitably must.

The development of advanced non-carbon energy technologies holds the promise of reducing the costs of atmospheric stabilization. While advanced technology does offer promise, its development is uncertain and the costs of reaching the levels assumed in this paper could be substantial. If the technologies assumed here do not come along as predicted in this study, then the costs of stabilization will be very substantial. The successful development and deployment of such technologies could eliminate the need for enforcement. The stabilization path would be enforced by the market. Firms using inefficient, high-emissions technologies would no longer be competitive. A variety of technologies both near at hand, and in their embryonic stage exist which could minimize the burden of transition to low and non-carbon emitting energy systems. Their rates of development and deployment will be affected by the level of United States energy R&D investment. As R&D is the classic example of under production due to market failure, increasing R&D easily falls within the realm of a "no regrets" action. Unfortunately, at present, United States energy R&D expenditure levels have been falling, and there is no good reason to believe that the trend will soon reverse on its own.

Footnotes

1. Of course, in long-term global mean temperatures will be identical for all paths leading to a common steady-state concentration.

2. Their result can be traced directly to two assumptions: the date at which uncertainty is resolved, the year 2020, and the minimum, "possible" ceiling, 400 ppmv. These two parameters alone determine the result in the decision analytic framework which they employed. The decision analytic framework requires that no option ever be foreclosed before the date of resolution of uncertainty. Thus, the model must preserve the option of a 400 ppmv ceiling until the year 2020 regardless of cost and regardless of the probability of occurrence. But the 400 ppmv ceiling is extremely tight. For it not to be violated before the year 2020 requires the model to behave as if it were the only ceiling. Any optimal deterministic emissions path for a steady-state level 450 ppmv or higher yields a concentration in excess of 400 ppmv before the year 2020. Thus, the decision analytic framework must choose a path close to the 400 ppmv path. But this is not a policy relevant insight. Ha-Duong, Grubb and Hourcade have simply pushed the decision analytical framework beyond its useful limits. Had they inserted a 1 in 10100 chance that the ceiling should be 360 ppmv, their model has no choice but to shut down all fossil energy use immediately and wait for the year 2020 at which date the uncertainty is resolved. Only in that year would the model have any chance of using fossil energy again. Note that the probability chosen is irrelevant. Only the date of resolution and the ceiling matter. Of course, if they had allowed ANY possibility of a 358 ppmv ceiling, a concentration which has already been surpassed, the model would not even solve.

3. Annex I is the group of nations: Australia, Austria, Belarus, Belgium, Bulgaria, Canada, Czechoslovakia, Denmark, European Economic Community, Estonia, Finland, France, Germany, Greece, Hungary, Iceland, Ireland, Italy, Japan, Latvia, Lithuania, Luxembourg, Netherlands, New Zealand, Norway, Poland, Portugal, Romania, Russian Federation, Spain, Sweden, Switzerland, Turkey, Ukraine, United Kingdom of Great Britain and Northern Ireland, and the United States.

4. We note that after the year 2025 Annex I percentage emissions reductions relative to IS92a exceed those of non-Annex I nations.

5. This observation goes under the name of the Hotelling Theorem.

6. As such it is a slight overestimate of the true minimum cost as it incorporates somewhat less mitigation in the early years than the WRE, and therefore would be associated with a somewhat lower concentration than the WRE.

7. Nanoscale is very small, 10-9 meters.

8. For example, microscale heat exchangers have shown transfer rates approaching 100 W/cm2 (Cuta et al, 1995).

9. For example, Fluid flow in 100 micron channels has very small temperature gradients and high surface contact, thus providing more intimate control of the efficiency of reactions. Such control is critical in energy applications such as partial oxidation reactors for methane reforming (Wegeng et al, 1996).

10. Efficient, low weight and portable chemical and energy systems are under development. Drost et al. (1996)

11. A variety of redundant, on demand and point of use chemical and energy systems seem possible. Wegeng et al. (1996).

References

Barns, D.W., J.A. Edmonds, and J.M. Reilly. 1992. *Use of the Edmonds-Reilly Model to Model Energy Related Greenhouse Gas Emissions for Inclusion in an OECD Survey Volume.* OECD-/GD(92)90, Economics Department Working Papers No. 113, Organization for Economic Cooperation and Development, Paris, FRANCE.

Chapuis, T., M. Ha-Duong, and M. Grubb. 1996. *DIAM: A Model for studying Dynamic Inertia and Adaptability in the climate change issue,* Submitted to *The Energy Journal.*

Cline, W.R. 1992. *The Economics of Global Warming.* Institute for International Economics, Washington, DC.

COP (The Conference of the Parties). 1995. *The Berlin Mandate: Decision 1/CP.1.* reprinted in The United Nations Climate Change Bulletin, Issue 2, 2nd Quarter 1995. Interim Secretariat of the UNEP/WMO Intergovernmental Panel on Climate Change (IPCC), and the UNEP/WMO Information Unit on Climate Change (IUCC), Geneva Executive Center, CP 356, 1219 Chatelaine, SWITZERLAND.

Cuta, J. M., A. Shekarriz and C.E. McDonald, 1996, "Forced Convection heat Transfer in Micro-Channel heat Exchangers" accepted for presentation at ASME Winter Annual Meeting, Atlanta, GA, November 1996.

DOE (United States Department of Energy). 1996. *Policies and Measures for Reducing Energy Related Greenhouse Gas Emissions.* DOE/EO-0047. National Technical Information Service, U.S. Department of Commerce, Springfield Virginia 22161.

Dooley, J. 1996. *Trends in US Private-Sector Energy R&D Funding 1985-1994.* PNNL-11295. Pacific

Northwest National Laboratory, Washington, DC. (24 pages)

Dowlatabadi, H. 1996. *Adaptive Strategies for Climate Change Mitigation: Implications for Policy Design and Timing.* Department of Engineering & Public Policy, Carnegie Mellon University, Pittsburgh.

Drost, M.K. and R.S. Wegeng, 1996, "Distributed Space Conditioning for Residential Applications" presented at 1996 Conference of The American Council for an Energy Efficient Economy.

Edmonds, J. and Reilly, J. 1985. *Global Energy: Assessing the Future,* Oxford University Press, New York, pp.317.

Edmonds, J.A., Reilly, J.M., Gardner, R.H., and Brenkert, A. 1986. *Uncertainty in Future Global Energy Use and Fossil Fuel CO_2 Emissions 1975 to 2075,* TR036, DO3/NBB-0081 Dist. Category UC-11, National Technical Information Service, U.S. Department of Commerce, Springfield Virginia 22161.

Edmonds, J., M. Wise, D. Barns. 1995. "Carbon Coalitions: The Cost and Effectiveness of Energy Agreements to Alter Trajectories of Atmospheric Carbon Dioxide Emissions," *Energy Policy,23*(4/5):309-336.

Edmonds, J., Wise, M., Pitcher, H., Richels, R., Wigley, T., and MacCracken, C. 1996. "An Integrated Assessment of Climate Change and the Accelerated Introduction of Advanced Energy Technologies: An Application of MiniCAM 1.0," *Environmental Modelling & Assessment,* (forthcoming).

Edmonds, J., M. Wise, R. Sands, R. Brown, and H. Kheshgi. 1996. *Agriculture, Land-Use, and Commercial Biomass Energy: A Preliminary Integrated Analysis of the Potential Role of Biomass Energy for Reducing Future Greenhouse Related Emissions.* PNNL-

11155. Pacific Northwest National Laboratories, Washington, DC.

Grubb, M. 1996a. *Technologies, Energy Systems, and the Timing of CO₂ Emissions Abatement: An Overview of Economic Issues.* Submitted to Energy Policy. Energy and Environmental Programme, Royal Institute of International Affairs, London SW1Y 4LE, United Kingdom.

Grubb, M. 1996b. *Economic and Environmental Choices in the Stabilization of Atmospheric CO₂ Concentrations: A Critical Review.* Energy and Environmental Programme, Royal Institute of International Affairs, London SW1Y 4LE, United Kingdom.

Grubb, M. T. Chapuis, and M.H. Duong. 1995. "The Economics of Changing Course: Implications of Adaptability and Inertia for Optimal Climate Policy," *Energy Policy.* 23(4):1-14.

Ha-Duong, M., Grubb, M., and J.-C. Hourcade. 1996. "Optimal Emission Paths Toward CO2 Stabilization and the Cost of Deferring Abatement: The Influence of Inertia and Uncertainty," submitted to *Nature.*

IPCC (Intergovernmental Panel on Climate Change), 1995. *Climate Change 1994: Radiative Forcing of Climate Change and An Evaluation of the IPCC IS92 Emissions Scenarios* J.T. Houghton, L.G.M. Filho, J. Bruce, H. Lee, B.A. Callander, E. Haites, N. Harris, and K. Maskell. (eds.), Cambridge University Press, Cambridge, United Kingdom.

IPCC (Intergovernmental Panel on Climate Change), 1996a. *Climate Change 1995: The Science of Climate Change. The Contribution of Working Group I to the Second Assessment Report of the Intergovernmental Panel on Climate Change.* J.P. Houghton, L.G. Meira Filho, B.A. Callendar, A. Kattenberg, and K. Maskell (eds.).

Cambridge University Press, Cambridge, UK.

IPCC (Intergovernmental Panel on Climate Change), 1992. *Climate Change 1992: The Supplementary Report to the IPCC Scientific Assessment.* J.T. Houghton, B.A. Callander and S.K. Varney (eds.), Cambridge University Press, Cambridge, United Kingdom.

IPCC (Intergovernmental Panel on Climate Change), 1996b. *Climate Change 1995: Impacts, Adaptation, and Mitigation of Climate Change: Scientific-Technical Analysis. The Contribution of Working Group II to the Second Assessment Report of the Intergovernmental Panel on Climate Change.* R.T. Watson, M.C. Zinyowera, R.H. Moss (eds.). Cambridge University Press, Cambridge, UK.

IPCC (Intergovernmental Panel on Climate Change), 1996c. *Climate Change 1995: Economic and Social Dimensions of Climate Change. The Contribution of Working Group III to the Second Assessment Report of the Intergovernmental Panel on Climate Change.* J.P. Bruce, H. Lee, and E.F. Haites (eds.). Cambridge University Press, Cambridge, UK.

Kolstad, C.D. 1994. "The Timing of CO2 Control in the Face of Uncertainty and Learning" in *International Environmental Economics.* E.C. Van Ierland, (ed.), pp.75-96, Elsevier, Amsterdam.

Kolstad, C.D. 1992. "Looking vs. Leaping: The Timing of CO2 Control in the Face of Uncertainty and Learning," in *Costs, Impacts, and Possible Benefits of CO₂ Mitigation,* Y. Kaya, N. Nakicenovic, W.D. Nordhaus, and F.L. Toth (eds.), the Institute for Applied Systems Analysis (IIASA), Laxenburg, AUSTRIA (June).

Leggett, J., W.J. Pepper, R.J. Swart, J. Edmonds, L.G. Meira Filho, I.

Mintzer, M.X. Wang, and J. Wasson. 1992. "Emissions Scenarios for the IPCC: An Update." in *Climate Change 1992: The Supplementary Report to the IPCC Scientific Assessment,* University Press, Cambridge, UK. Change.

Manne, A.S., R. Mendelsohn, R. Richels. 1995. "MERGE — A Model for Evaluating Regional and Global Effects of GHG Reduction Policies." *Energy Policy, 23*(1):17-34.

Manne, A.S. and R.G. Richels. 1993. *CO₂ Hedging Strategies — the Impact of Uncertainty Upon Emissions,* draft paper for presentation at the OECD/IEA Conference on the Economics of Climate Change, in Paris, June 14-16, 1993.

Nordhaus, W.D. 1994. *Managing the Global Commons: The Economics of Climate Change.* MIT Press, Cambridge, MA.

Peck, S.C. and T.J. Teisberg. 1994. "Optimal Carbon Emissions Trajectories When Damages Depend of the Rate or Level of Warming," *The Energy Journal, 30*:289-314.

Richels, R., J. Edmonds, H. Gruenspecht, and T. Wigley. 1996. *The Berlin Mandate: The Design of Cost-Effective Mitigation Strategies.* Energy Modeling Forum Subgroup on Regional Distribution of the Costs and Benefits of Climate Change Policy Proposals report. Stanford, CA.

Teich, A.H. 1996. Director, Science and Policy Programs, American Association for the Advancement of Science, Testimony before the U.S. House of Representatives' Science Committee July 23, 1996.

Wegeng, R.S., C.J. Call and M.K. Drost, 1996, "Chemical Systems Miniaturization" presented at the 1996 AIChE Spring National Meeting, February 1996.

Wigley, T.M.L., R. Richels & J. A. Edmonds. 1996. "Economic and Environmental Choices in the Stabilization of Atmospheric CO_2 Concentrations," *Nature. 379*(6562): 240-243.

Appendix IV
Transportation Technology Trends

Trevor O. Jones
Chairman of the Board, Echlin, Inc.

Trevor Jones also serves as the Chairman of the National Research Council Standing Committee to Review the Partnership for a New Generation of Vehicles (PNGV) and his views expressed herein do not necessarily represent the views of the National Academy of Science, the National Research Council, or any of its constituents.

Appendix IV—Table of Contents

Introduction

It is an honor and a pleasure to be invited to your Forum, *2020 Vision: The Energy World in the Next Century*. Dr. Jack Gibbons has asked me to briefly discuss Transportation Technology Trends.

It is generally accepted that the principle source of transportation energy for the next 25 years will be petroleum, which will be combusted in some form of energy converter with resulting emissions. Due to the dramatic anticipated increases in global transportation vehicles, fuel economy, total energy consumption and engine emissions, within the context of sound economic principles, will be the dominant factors in future transportation vehicle and propulsion system designs. As we pursue even more energy efficient and lower emitting vehicles, we will need to resort to more radical designs.

Without doubt, the next 25 years will be an intense, challenging and exciting technologically driven period for transportation vehicles in a highly competitive global market.

As this audience is fully aware, in 1995, on-highway vehicles used 74% of the total transportation energy consumed, air was second at 13%, marine 7% and rail 2%. This pattern is not expected to change dramatically over the next two decades,

---

Editor's note: Due to space limitations, the section of this paper on civil aviation is not reprinted here.

FIGURE 1

TRANSPORTATION ENERGY USE BY MODE
(Quadrillion Btu per year)

MODE	1995 Use	%	2010 Use	%	2015 Use	%
Light Duty Vehicles	14.20	58.4	17.26	55.5	17.43	54.0
Freight Trucks	3.86	15.9	4.99	16.0	5.18	16.0
SUBTOTAL	**18.06**	**74.3**	**22.25**	**71.5**	**22.61**	**70.0**
Air	3.18	13.1	4.71	15.1	5.00	15.5
Rail	0.48	2.0	0.51	1.6	0.51	1.6
Marine	1.63	6.7	2.30	7.4	2.46	7.6
Pipeline & Other	0.93	3.8	1.17	3.8	1.23	3.8
Transportation Energy	**24.31**	**100**[1]	**31.11**	**100**	**31.99**	**100**
TOTAL ENERGY	**90.83**	**26.8**	**103.36**	**28.4**	**110.87**	**28.9**

NOTE: (1) Percentages will have rounding errors.

Source: Energy Information Administration. Annual Energy Outlook 1997. Table A-7 Reference Case Forecast, Page 107.

however, it is predicted that on-road fuel consumption will drop by 4%, and air will increase two and a half percent[1].

Though alternate fuels and alternate fuel vehicles are being developed, petroleum will be the dominant transportation fuel for the next quarter of a century, which is forecasted to be 95% in 2015[1]. The major barriers to the introduction of alternate fuel vehicles are more economic and infrastructure driven than the need for basic vehicle inventions. In the interest of time, Dr. Joan Ogden will cover alternate transportation fuels in her presentation this morning.

To complete this backdrop on transportation energy, we should add that:

- Transportation accounted for 27% of total U.S. energy consumption in 1995 and is projected to increase to 29% by 2015.

- Transportation accounted for 67% of total petroleum consumed in USA in 1995 and is projected to increase to 70% by 2015.

- Net petroleum imports are projected to increase from 44% in 1995 to 61% by 2015.

- The transportation sector produced 33% of total U.S. carbon emissions in 1995 and is projected to be 34% in 2015.

Given these statistics, it is clearly obvious that a quantum reduction in transportation energy consumption must be achieved on a global basis through conservation and the development and application of new technologies.

FIGURE 2

TRANSPORTATION ENERGY SOURCES
(Quadrillion Btu per year)

source	1995	2005	2010	2015
Petroleum	23.56	28.22	29.69	30.39
Pipeline Fuel Ng	0.72	0.84	0.88	0.93
Compressed Ng	0.01	0.18	0.26	0.31
Renewable Energy (E85)	0.00	0.02	0.07	0.10
Methanol	0.00	0.03	0.07	0.09
Liquid Hydrogen	0.00	0.00	0.00	0.00
Electricity	0.02	0.08	0.14	0.17
Electricity Losses	0.04	0.17	0.28	0.32
Transportation Energy	**24.36**	**29.55**	**31.39**	**32.32**
Total Energy	**90.83**	**103.36**	**107.89**	**110.87**
% Transportation	**26.8**	**28.6**	**29.1**	**29.2**

Source: Energy Information Administration. Annual Energy Outlook, 1997. Table C-2 Reference Case, Page 154.

FIGURE 3

TRANSPORTATION ENERGY USAGE

- Transportation accounted for 27% of total U.S. Energy consumption in 1995 and is projected to increase to 29% by 2015.

- Transportation accounted for 67% of total petroleum consumed in USA in 1995 and is projected to increase to 70% by 2015.

- Net petroleum imports projected to increase from 44% in 1995 to 61% by 2015.

- Transportation (all fuels) produced 33% of total U.S. carbon emissions in 1995 and is projected to be 34% in 2015.

Source: Energy Information Administration, Annual Energy Outlook, 1997. Figure 94 and Tables A-7, C-2 & C-19 Reference Case.

FIGURE 4

PROJECTED ANNUAL GROWTH IN TRANSPORTATION ENERGY USE AND IMPROVEMENTS IN ENERGY EFFICIENCY 1995-2015

| | HIGHWAY VEHICLES | | AIR | MARINE | RAIL |
	LIGHT	HEAVY			
ANNUAL GROWTH IN ENERGY USE %	1.0	1.3	2.3	2.1	0.3
ANNUAL ENERGY EFFICIENCY %	0.4	0.4	0.9	0.5	1.0

Source: Energy Information Administration, Annual Energy Outlook, 1997. Reference Case Table A-7.

This situation is further aggravated because, with the exception of rail, it is predicted that all modes of transportation will increase energy consumption at a faster rate than improvements in energy efficiency. It is also forecasted that the worldwide on-highway vehicle park will double to in excess of 1.3 billion vehicles and air travel demand will triple in the next two decades.

While I will devote the majority of my presentation to light duty on-highway vehicles and air transportation technology trends, it is of interest to note that all vehicles for all modes have a common set of design parameters when considering energy efficiency as shown below:

- Total vehicle operating efficiency.
- Thermal efficiency of energy converter.
- Vehicle weight.
- Aerodynamic drag.
- Emissions.
- Safety.
- Fuel flexibility.
- Serviceability.
- Cost of construction.
- Economics of operation.

To this list we must add transportation system operating efficiency, which is the impact of traffic delays due to: congestion, traffic volume, road construction, inadequate traffic control, inclement weather conditions, accidents, etc., etc.

In this regard, the continuing research, development and deployment of intelligent highway systems, improved air traffic control systems, improved real time weather forecasting and all weather aircraft operating systems, is essential if we are to optimize transportation energy efficiency.

U.S. Light Duty On-highway Vehicles

I would first like to discuss on-highway light vehicle technology trends since they consume about 60% of the total transportation fuels. There is great concern around the world because improvements in new light vehicle fuel economy have plateaued. Figure 5 shows this trend for the average new U.S., Japanese and European fleets for the past 24 years.

FIGURE 5

U.S. AVERAGE NEW CAR FLEET FUEL ECONOMY VERSUS JAPAN AND OTHER OECD COUNTRIES, 1970–1994

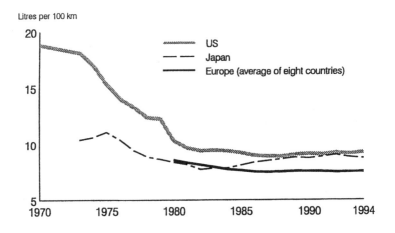

Source: Energy Use and Efficiency: Understanding the Links between Energy and Human Activity. International Energy Agency (IEA), Paris, 1997.

An interesting observation is that there essentially is no difference between U.S. and Japanese new vehicle fleets (Figure 6). The higher level of fuel economy for European cars is partly due to higher usage of diesel powered vehicles. Over the past decade the fuel economy for these three geographic areas has remained between 7.5 & 9.5 Liters/km, which translates into 25 to 32 mpg.

The plateauing of fuel economy improvement led the U.S. government in 1992 to commission the NRC to examine automotive fuel economy and determine the technically feasible upper limit over the next decade.

The results of the NRC study are[2] shown on Figures 6 and 7 with high and low confidence levels for Model Year 2006. Also shown are the estimated incremental retail prices for these two levels of fuel economy improvement.

FIGURE 6

"TECHNICALLY ACHIEVABLE" FUEL ECONOMY LEVELS
FOR MYS 1996, 2001 & 2006

VEHICLE SIZE CLASS	MY 1996	FUEL ECONOMY (MPG)			
		MY 2001		MY 2006	
		Higher Confidence	Lower Confidence	Higher Confidence	Lower Confidence
Passenger Cars					
Subcompact	32	36	38	39	44
Compact	30	32	34	34	38
Midsize	27	29	31	32	35
Large	24	27	29	30	33
New Car Fleet	29	31	33	34	37
Light Trucks					
Small pickup	26	28	29	29	32
Small van	24	26	27	28	30
Small utility	22	24	25	26	29
Large pickup	20	22	23	23	25
New Light-Truck Fleet					
	22	24	25	26	28

NOTES: The new-car and light-truck average fuel economy by size class for MY 1996 assumes 0.7 mpg improvement in each size class from its corresponding EPA composite average level in MY 1991. This assumption is similar to that made by SRI (1991) for MY 1995 vehicles starting from a MY 1990 base.

Fuel economy values by size class shown for MY 2001 were obtained by interpolation between values for MY 1996 and MY 2006.

The new-car and light-truck fleet average fuel economies are shown above for illustrative purposes and are calculated assuming a size-class mix similar to that for MY 1990 vehicles, as follows: passenger cars — subcompact, 23 percent; compact, 35 percent; midsize, 26 percent; large, 16 percent; light trucks — small pickup, 15 percent; small van, 29 percent; small utility, 16 percent; large pickup, 40 percent. Data are based on Heavenrich et al. (1991)

Source: Automotive Fuel Economy: How Far Should We Go? National Research Council Report, 1992. Table 8-2.

FIGURE 7

"TECHNICALLY ACHIEVABLE" FUEL ECONOMY LEVELS FOR MY 2006 VEHICLES

Vehicle Size Class	Ranges of "Technically Achievable" Fuel Economy in MY 2006ᵃ/(mpg)		Incremental Retail Price Equivalent for Improved Fuel Economy in MY 2006ᵇ/ (1990 Dollars)	
	Higher Confidence	Lower Confidence	At Higher Confidence Fuel Economy	At Lower Confidence Fuel Economy
Passenger Cars				
Subcompact	39	44	500–1,250	1,000–2,500
Compact	34	38	500–1,250	1,200–2,500
Midsize	32	35	500–1,250	1,000–2,500
Large	30	33	500–1,250	1,000–2,500
Light Trucks				
Small pickup	29	32	500–1,000	1,000–2,000
Small van	28	30	500–1,250	1,000–2,500
Small utility	26	29	500–1,250	1,250–2,500
Large pickup	23	25	750–1,750	1,500–2,750

NOTES: ᵃ/ The term "technically achievable" is circumscribed by the following assumptions made by the committee. The estimates result from consideration of technologies currently used in vehicles mass produced somewhere in the world and that pay for themselves at gasoline prices of $5.00 to $10.00 per gallon or less (1990 dollars). The estimates assume compliance with applicable known safety standards and Tier I emissions requirements of the Clean Air Act amendments of 1990. Compliance with Tier II and California's emissions standards has not been taken into account. The estimates also assume that MY 2006 vehicles will have the acceleration performance of, and meet customer requirements for functionality equivalent to, 1990 models. The estimates take into account past trends in vehicle fuel economy improvements and evidence from "best-in-class" fuel economy experience. The term "technically achievable" should not be taken to mean the technological limits of what is possible with the current state of the art; nor should the committee's estimates of what is technically achievable be taken as its recommendations as to what future fuel economy levels should be.

Aside from the limits imposed by the foregoing assumptions, no cost-benefit considerations entered into the determination of the technically achievable fuel economy levels. Specifically, the estimates do not take into account other factors that should be considered by policymakers in determining any future fuel economy regulations, including impacts on the competitiveness of automotive and related industries, sales and employment effects, petroleum import dependance, effects on nonregulated emissions (e.g., the greenhouse gas, carbon dioxide); and the development and adoption of unanticipated technology.

As a point of reference, the Environmental Protection Agency's (EPA's) composite average fuel economy for MY 1990 passenger cars and light trucks, by size class, was as follows: passenger cards — subcompact, 31.4 mpg; compact, 29.4; midsize, 26.1; large, 23.5; light trucks — small pickup, 25.7; small van, 22.8; small utility, 21.3; large pickup, 19.1 (Heavenrich et al., 1991).

ᵇ/ The retail price equivalents are estimates only of the incremental first cost to consumers of improved fuel economy. They do not include incremental costs associated with mandated improvements to occupant safety, which, on average for new passenger cars and light trucks, are expected to be $300 and $500, respectively in 1990 dollars; nor do they include incremental costs of controls to comply with Tier I emissions requirements, which are expected to range from a few hundred dollars to $1,600 per vehicle.

On a new passenger car fleet basis for model year 2006, the estimated technically achievable fuel economy is between 34 and 37mpg. This represents a 24 to 35% increase over today's 27.5 mpg, CAFE standard. In a similar manner, a 26 to 35% increase is estimated over the light vehicle standard of 20.7mpg. The retail incremental price increase is $500 - $1250 for the high confidence fuel economy level and $1000 - $2500 for the lower confidence level for cars. The corresponding values for light trucks are $500 - $1750 and $1000 - $2750, respectively (Figure 8). Given that these price estimates are in 1990 dollars, it is unlikely that the average consumer would get a positive payback with an average vehicle life of 8 to 9 years, gasoline at $1.25 per gallon and driving 12,500 miles annually with these incremental fuel economy improvements.

Figures 8 and 9 provide an indication of the types of incremental changes and related costs which were considered for subcompact cars in the NRC study. As can be seen, the majority of changes encompass the power train (engine and transmission) and vehicle weight reduction. The fuel economy tends towards an asymptotic level of 39 to 44mpg which is what the nrc study concluded for high and low confidence levels for MY 2006 subcompacts.

Following the 1992 NCR report, it became obvious that with the anticipated large increase in the number of vehicles in operation over the next two decades, the incremental approach would be insufficient to stem the tide of increasing transportation fuel consumption and the corresponding impact on air quality.

In September, 1993, President Clinton and the CEOs of the Detroit Big Three announced and launched the U.S. industry/government partnership for a new generation of vehicles (PNGV) [3].

The objectives of this program are:

Goal 1   Significantly improve national competitiveness in manufacturing for future generations of vehicles.

Goal 2   Implement commercially viable innovations from ongoing research on conventional vehicles.

FIGURE 8

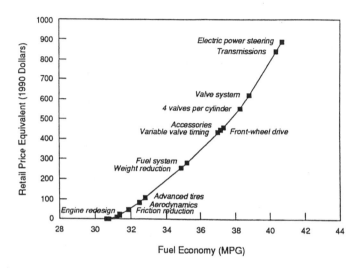

CALCULATION OF FUEL ECONOMY COSTS
FOR SUBCOMPACT CARS

Source: Automotive Fuel Economy: How Far Should We Go? National Research Council Report, 1992. Figure E-1.

Goal 3 Develop vehicles to achieve up to three times the fuel efficiency of comparable 1994 family sedans.

The main thrust of the program is Goal 3 with the following objectives, as related to a 1994 family sedan:

- Up to 3x fuel economy (80mpg) of 1994 Taurus/Lumina/ Concorde size car.

- Maintain or improve performance.

- Maintain size and utility.

- Maintain total cost of ownership - adjusted for economics.

- Meet or exceed promulgated federal safety and emission requirements.

- Selection of promising technologies by end of 1997.

FIGURE 9

CALCULATION OF FUEL ECONOMY COSTS FOR SUBCOMPACT CARS

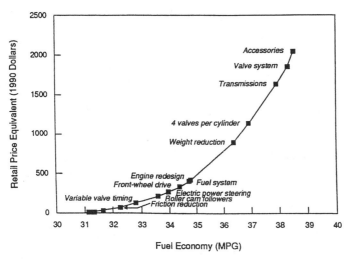

Source: Automotive Fuel Economy: How Far Should We Go? National Research Council Report, 1992. Figure E-1.

FIGURE 10

PNGV RELATIONSHIPS

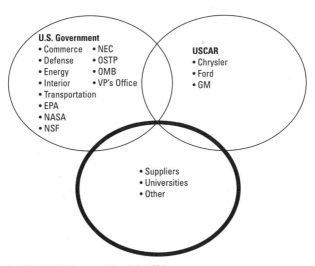

Source: Section 10—PNGV Program Plan, July 1994

FIGURE 11

ENERGY DISTRIBUTION IN A TYPICAL AUTOMOBILE

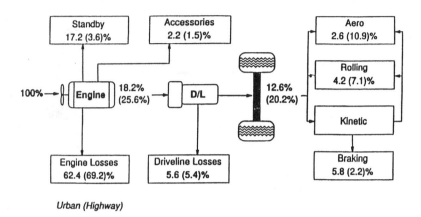

Urban (Highway)

Source: Figure 5-1, Partnership for a New Generation Vehicle — PNGV Program Plan, July 1994

FIGURE 12

ACHIEVING "3X" FUEL ECONOMY REQUIRES MAJOR IMPROVE-MENTS IN ALL POWERTRAIN AND VEHICLE CHARACTERISTICS

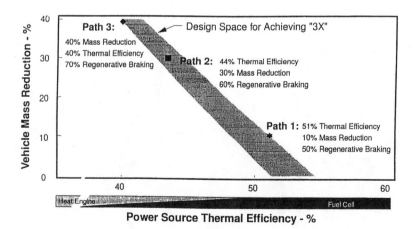

Note: All paths include: 90% efficient energy storage, 76.5% efficient driveline, 20% lower drag, 20% lower rolling resistance, 30% lower accessories loads.

Source: Inventions Needed for PNGV. August, 1996. Figure 2.

- Produce concept vehicles by 2000.

- Produce production prototypes by 2004.

The 80mpg goal for PNGV is extremely tough and will be pursued as a joint development effort by departments of the federal government's national laboratories, USCAR (the Big 3's Consortium to develop pre-competitive technologies), suppliers and universities.

In its initial evaluation, PNGV ruled out the straight electrical vehicle on the basis that it could not meet the cost and range requirements within the time constraints of the program. Other concerns included life of battery, cost of replacing battery, charging time and availability of charging facilities.

Likewise, the spark ignited gasoline engine (SIGE) was ruled out because of its inability to meet PNGV fuel economy and emission targets.

In order to achieve the very ambitious fuel economy goal, every single part of the vehicle will be investigated for potential improvement. Figure 11 shows the energy distribution in a typical automobile on urban and highway driving cycles. It is interesting to note that in city driving that only 12.6% of the equivalent energy in the tank reaches the wheels.

FIGURE 13

GOAL 3: TYPICAL IMPROVEMENTS OBJECTIVES

- Double thermal efficiency to 40% - 55%
- Reduce weight by 10% - 40%
- Capture 50% to 70% of braking energy
- Reduce drag by 20%
- Reduce rolling resistance by 20%
- Lower accessories loads by 30%

Source: Inventions Needed for PGNV, August 1996

The largest energy consumer is engine losses at almost 70% for highway driving, hence, the vital interest in improving thermal efficiency.

Figure 12 shows the basic trade-off envelope of weight reduction and improvements in thermal efficiency of energy conversion system to achieve 80mpg (3L/km). The envelope covers a thermal efficiency of approximately 40 to 55%, which is about twice as efficient as current engines.

In order to achieve 80mpg for the mid-size car at a thermal efficiency of 40%, a weight reduction of about 40% would be required. Likewise, a thermal efficiency of 55% could be achieved with a weight reduction of about 10%.

The design envelope assumes a high degree of regenerative braking from 50 to 70% and a 90% efficient energy storage, 76.5% efficient driveline, 20% lower drag, 20% lower rolling resistance and 30% lower accessories loads.

The major areas of development are:

- Hybrid electric power trains

  - Diesel Engine

  - Gas Turbine

  - Stirling Engine

- Fuel Cell - electric power trains

  - Fuel Processing

  - Proton-Exchange Membrane

- Energy Storage Devices

  - Mechanical

  - Electro-chemical

- Electrical/Electronic Power Control Systems

- Ultra light weight materials

- Lower Aerodynamic Drag

- Lower Rolling Resistance Tires

FIGURE 14

FORD P2000 HYBRID VEHICLE WEIGHT

POUNDS	1997 TAURUS	P2000	% MASS REDUCTION
Body	1571	875	44
Chassis	813	478	40
Powertrain	794	569	28
Fuel	140	78	44
TOTAL	**3318**	**2000**	**40**

Source: Ford Motor Company, March 17, 1997

FIGURE 15

FORD P2000 HYBRID VEHICLE WEIGHT

POUNDS	1997 TAURUS	P2000
FERROUS	2155	490
ALUMINUM	284	733
MAGNESIUM	10	86
TITANIUM	0	11
PLASTIC	381	270
RUBBER	146	123
CARBON FIBER	0	8
GLASS	93	36
LEXAN	0	30
OTHER	249	213
TOTAL	3318	2000

Source: Ford Motor Company, March 17, 1997

FIGURE 16

FORD P2000 DIATA POWERTRAIN

- DIATA - Direct Injection, Aluminum, Through-Bolt Assembly

- 1.2 Liter 4 Cylinder 55KW CIDI Engine

- 40% Thermal Efficiency

- Aluminum Cylinder Walls with Cast-Iron Liners

- 5 Speed Automatic Transmission

Source: Ford Motor Company, March 17, 1997s

Significant progress has been made by PNGV on a broad front which will lead to the selection of promising technologies by the end of 1997[4].

An example of the progress on weight reduction is the ongoing development of the ford P2000 hybrid electric mid-size car (Figure 14). The P2000 has actually achieved a 40% weight reduction from today's Taurus.

This 40% weight reduction has been achieved mainly through the expanded use of aluminum and to some extent, magnesium. The ferrous content of the P2000 has dropped by more than 1600 pounds or about 80% from the Taurus levels (Figure 15).

The power train for the Ford P2000 is a hybrid diesel electric, with a 40% thermal efficiency (Figure 16). The diesel engine is 1.2 liter four cylinder with a 5 speed automatic transmission. The P2000 is expected to achieve a fuel economy in excess of 50mpg.

If we compare the Ford P2000 with the PNGV design envelope, we can see that the 40% weight reduction and 40% thermal efficiency is about at the Path 3 point (Figure 17).

The major challenges at this time for a commercial hybrid diesel electric vehicle are:

FIGURE 17

ACHIEVING "3X" FUEL ECONOMY REQUIRES MAJOR IMPROVEMENTS IN ALL POWERTRAIN AND VEHICLE CHARACTERISTICS

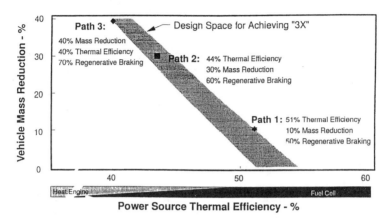

Note: All paths include: 90% efficient energy storage, 76.5% efficient driveline, 20% lower drag, 20% lower rolling resistance, 30% lower accessories loads

Source: Inventions Needed for PNGV. August, 1996. Figure 2.

- Added cost of a hybrid power train.

- Added cost of lightweight materials over steel.

- Added cost of a high speed direct injected fuel injection and control system.

- The development of a NO_x catalyst.

- The control of particulate matter.

- The development of a low cost and low weight energy storage system.

On a global basis, including PNGV, there is tremendous interest in fuel cells because of their high thermal efficiency and low emissions compared to combustion engines. The major challenges to be overcome in order to commercialize the system are first, technology developments leading to improved performance and greatly reduced production cost and second, a fueling infrastructure strategy.

At the present time cost is an enormous challenge. The PNGV target cost for the entire fuel-cell power plant is $50/kw while some current estimates indicate a production cost of more than $1000/kw. In early June 1997, a Daimler-Benz executive stated that today's gas and diesel engines cost 20-30 DM/kw and fuel cells cost 10,000 DM/kw. He further stated that fuel cells will not be commercialized before 2005 and 2010. Work is continuing on all aspects of the fuel-cell in order to reduce its cost and improve its performance, particularly in the areas of power, density and efficiency.

The other major challenge is fueling infrastructure. The fuel-cell works extremely well on hydrogen which is difficult to store on board a light duty vehicle in any form. Likewise, there is no economic infrastructure for the production, distribution and retailing of hydrogen on an extremely large scale as is the case for gasoline. These problems have motivated fuel-cell developers to design and evaluate reformers which derive hydrogen from methanol or gasoline. While this overcomes a large infrastructure problem, it does result in lower thermal efficiency and higher emissions.

The current PNGV approach to achieving its targets is to investigate a wide range of applicable technologies and to select the most promising by the end of 1997. While the selection process has not been completed, it would appear that initially the power train of choice will be a hybrid-electric system using a heat engine and then ultimately transition to an all-electric power train using fuel cells.

Emission reduction and control and choice of fuels are fundamental and integral parts of PNGV's analysis of the potential of each powertrain concept. Preliminary summary conclusions of the effects of various fuels and powertrains on emissions as presented[4] by Argonne National Laboratory and Volpe National Transportation Center are shown in Figure 18.

A basic consideration is whether the fuel cell powertrain can be successfully developed and commercialized with its superior

FIGURE 18

EFFECTS OF VARIOUS FUELS AND POWER PLANTS ON EMISSIONS

VOLATILE ORGANIC COMPOUNDS
- Fuel cells offer the greatest benefit
- Diesel fuel is similar to alternative fuels.

CARBON MONOXIDE
- Fuel cells offer the greatest benefit.
- Diesel fuel and dimethyl ether promise significant CO reductions.
- Alcohol fuels increase CO emissions.

OXIDES OF NITROGEN
- Hydrogen fuel cells offer the greatest benefit.
- Diesel and DME fuels could increase emissions.

PARTICULATE MATTER
- Fuel cells provide the most reduction.
- Emissions reductions also occur with reformulated gasoline, DME and methanol.
- Diesel fuel and ethanol fuel use increase particulate emissions.

SULFUR OXIDES
- Renewable fuels provide the greatest emissions reduction.
- Reformulated gasoline and diesel fuel provide some reductions, but not as much as dimethyl ether and methanol.

Source: NRC-Standing Committee to review the PNGV Research Program. Third PNGV Report, March, 1977.

thermal efficiency and low emissions prior to the successful development of a commercially competitive electric vehicle or a cost effective hybrid-electric vehicle.

European Light Duty On-Highway Vehicles

On June 1, 1995, the European Union, nudged by PNGV, launched the car of tomorrow task force to develop a competitive car for the future by 2003 - 2005.

FIGURE 19

EUROPEAN CAR OF TOMORROW

- Advanced energy storage and propulsion technologies, with emphasis on batteries and fuel cells.

- Essential accompanying technologies — electronics, lightweight materials, telematics (intelligent cars), etc.

- Combining these technologies in zero-emission or hybrid vehicles in close cooperation with representative of the motor industry.

- Integrating the new propulsion systems into new car systems.

Source: European Commission Task Force "Car of Tomorrow" Newsletter No. 0, Summer, 1995.

This action is in addition to a 1995 European Commission proposal which set fuel economy targets for new cars in Europe to achieve 5 liters/100km (48mpg) for gasoline powered vehicles and 4.5 (53mpg) for diesels by 2005. The ultimate European target is the same as PNGV of 3 liters per 100km, although the size class of the vehicle may be different. Since there are no CAFE standards in Europe, various governments are considering a number of additional taxes on fuel, vehicles with lower fuel economies and on level of carbon emissions.

The Car of Tomorrow Task Force has the responsibility to coordinate the highly fragmented efforts being made in Europe to develop more efficient, low and/or zero emission vehicles. The emphasis will be on the critical technological factors limiting the rapid development of such vehicles, particularly those shown in Figure 19.

At the same time, the European Union also established similar additional transportation related task forces, for example:

- New-generation aircraft
- Trains and railway systems of the future
- Intermodal transport
- Maritime systems of the future

The Commission decided to create these task forces in order to concentrate research efforts on topics which are essential for competitiveness of the European industry, employment and quality of life.

The Car of Tomorrow Task Force has established the following guidelines for deliverables:

Short to Medium Term

- Energy efficient, competitive ultra low and near zero emission vehicles (ULEV) vehicles for both urban and regional use, incorporating ultra-low emission combustion engines and cleaner fuels;

- Radically new, competitive, safe, intelligent, energy efficient, zero emission vehicle (ZEV) concepts, such as ultra compact electric vehicles (EV) for urban use;

Long Term

- Radical, fully sustainable, negligible or zero emission propulsion systems (for example fuel cells), which have the prospect of exploiting renewable primary energy sources.

The principle differences between the U.S.-PNGV and the European Car of Tomorrow are:

- The development of an ultra-compact car for urban use in addition to a vehicle for both urban and regional use.

- The development of electric vehicles.

- Exploitation of renewable primary energy sources.

- Very close coordination with energy supply industry.

In terms of comparing European, American and Japanese automotive technology on a general basis, I would suggest that a state of technological equivalence exists. In specific areas there are cases where one region is ahead or behind the other, but not in a dramatic way. One preliminary assessment of advanced automotive technologies was provided in the second nrc PNGV report[5] as shown on this slide, which indicates that there is no clear leader in all technologies. Though no rating

FIGURE 20

PRELIMINARY RANKING OF U.S., EUROPEAN AND JAPANESE ADVANCED AUTOMOTIVE TECHNOLOGIES

TECHNOLOGY	U.S.	EUROPE	JAPAN
Internal combustion,	3	1	2
compression ignition engine	2	2	1
Internal combustion, spark-ignition engine	2	2	1
Gas turbine	1 (systems)	1 (systems)	1 (components)
Fuel cell	Immature technology — no ratings assigned		
Flywheel	1	1	3
Battery	1 (high energy)	2	1 (high-power)
Ultracapacitor	3	3	1
Lightweight materials steel)	2	1 (aluminum)	1 (high-strengt

Note: 1 = highest ranking; 3 = lowest ranking

Source: NRC PNGV Review Review. March, 1996.

was provided for fuel cells, it is known that major developments are being pursued quite aggressively on a global basis.

In Europe, the energy companies, the vehicle builders and the legislatures formed a European Auto Oil Program to determine vehicle emissions controls for 2000 and 2005 as well as new legislation on fuel quality. Auto oil is based on three core principles:

- Linking further legislation to air quality targets.

- Looking at the whole vehicle - fuel system.

- Choosing the most cost-effective options.

Japanese Light Duty On-highway Vehicles

The Japanese have similar long-range development activities which emulate the technology scope of U.S.-PNGV and the European Car of Tomorrow programs. The Japanese programs appear to be more decentralized and essentially operate on a company by company basis. A major difference between the various regional programs is that the Japanese are pursuing direct-injected, spark ignited gasoline engines with more fervor than their international competitors.

In September 1996, Japan launched Japan's Clean Air Program (JCAP) in cooperation with MITI, the Petroleum Association of Japan (PAJ) and the Japan Automobile Manufacturers' Association (JAMA). The program objectives are:

- Clarify the mid- to long-term orientation of automobile and fuel technologies which reduce environmental loads to as low as can reasonably be achieved;

- Research into the effects of automobile and fuel technologies on vehicle emissions;

- Develop the next generation of clean automobile and fuel technologies;

- Propose a set of cost-effective automobile and fuel technology measures to improve air quality.

Conclusions

We have comfort that the industrialized world is focused on producing transportation vehicles that are dramatically more energy efficient with lower emissions than current vehicles. However, we have concerns that the introduction of new technologies will escalate vehicle acquisition cost and the extended development time to get these new vehicles to the market. Concurrently, the increasing global demand for transportation continues at a faster pace than our ability to introduce new energy and emissions reducing technologies.

In terms of transportation technology trends, there are some remarkable similarities which cut across all future vehicle designs; I will mention some of these technologies which are being developed for introduction in future vehicles:

- Traditional and non-traditional power plants with substantially improved thermal efficiency.

- The precise control of the combustion process to achieve ultra-low emissions and the design of after-treatment devices where applicable.

- The specification, production and blending of fuels to permit optimization of engine performance and low emissions.

- engines and vehicles designed to use alternate fuels where fuel quality, fuel availability and economics can be guaranteed.

- The continual reduction of weight through the use of lightweight high strength steels, aluminum, magnesium, titanium, and composites.

- The ability to continuously conduct on-board diagnostics (OBD) of a wide range of engine and vehicle parameters.

- An extremely large expansion in the use of microprocessors, power electronics, fiber optics, sensors, actuators and electronic displays.

- The implementation of electronic drive or fly by wire systems for all engine and vehicle controls to improve performance and enhance safety.

- The optimization of the total electrical and electronic systems and the standardization of interfaces.

- The concurrent development of new manufacturing processes for the wide range of new 2020 technologies to be employed.

It is essential that parallel developments continue which address the efficiency of integrated transportation systems for land, air and sea. These developments include intelligent transportation system for highway traffic, air traffic control, reliable real-time weather forecasting and a host of digital communication systems.

It would also be beneficial if transportation technology development organizations established a forum for the exchange of applicable information with colleagues in other transportation sectors.

Thank you.

Acknowledgements

I wish to acknowledge the kind and willing support provided me by Calvin Watson, the Boeing Company, Leland Coons, Pratt & Whitney, Brian Rowe and Ambrose Hauser, GE Aircraft Engines and Douglas Bauer, James Zucchetto and Thomas Menzies of the National Research Council.

References

1. Annual Energy Outlook—1997. Energy Information Administration. December 1996.

2. Automotive Fuel Economy; How Far Should We Go? National Research Council, 1992.

3. Program Plan, Partnership for a New Generation of Vehicles (PNGV). November 29, 1995.

4. Review of the Research Program of the Partnership for a New Generation of Vehicles—Third Report. NRC, March 1997.

5. Review of the Research Program of the Partnership for a New Generation of Vehicles—Second Report. NRC, March 1996.

Trevor Jones also serves as the Chairman of the National Research Council Standing Committee to Review the Partnership for a New Generation of Vehicles (PNGV) and his views expressed herein do not necessarily represent the views of the National Academy of Sciences, the National Research Council, or any of its constituent units.

Appendix V
Royal Dutch/Shell Energy Scenarios

Roger Rainbow
Shell International Limited

Aspen Energy Policy Forum
Session 4: Market Structures

ROYAL DUTCH/SHELL ENERGY SCENARIOS

Roger Rainbow
Shell International Limited

Aspen
8th July, 1997

FIGURE 1

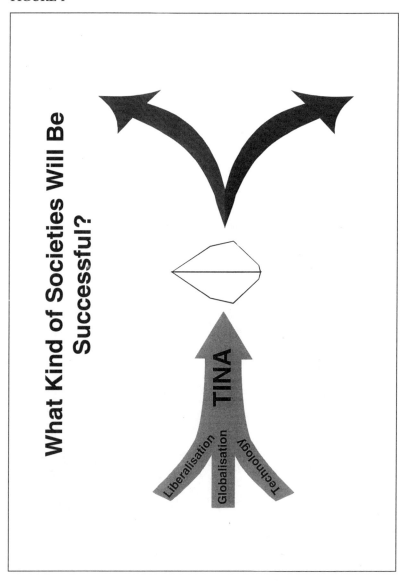

FIGURE 2

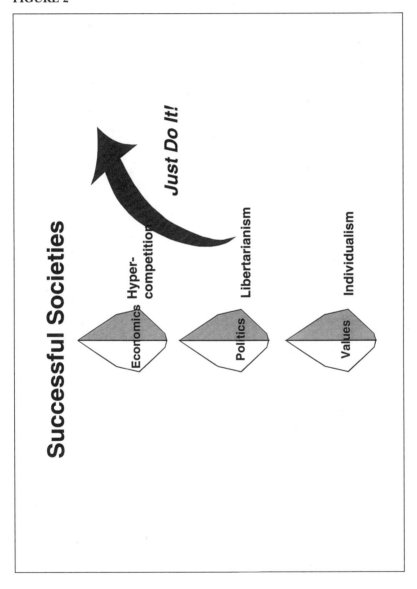

FIGURE 3

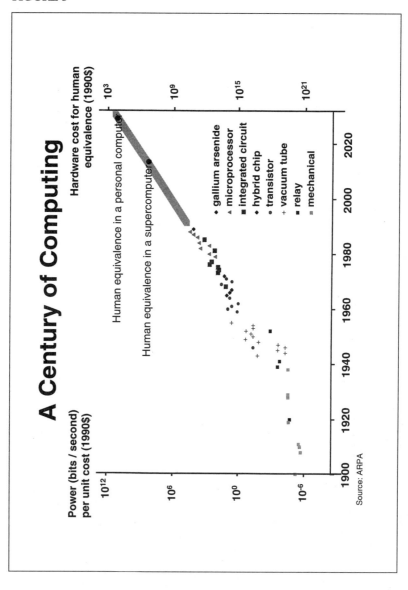

FIGURE 4

I.T. and the Energy Business

- Virtuality (from atoms to bits)
  - Communications and Travel
  - Office and Energy
- Details of Information
  - End of Statistics
  - Customer Characterisation
  - Seismic
- Intelligent Appliances
  - Domestic Meters
  - Control and Logistics
- Expert Systems
  - Design (speed and complexity)
  - Operations

FIGURE 5

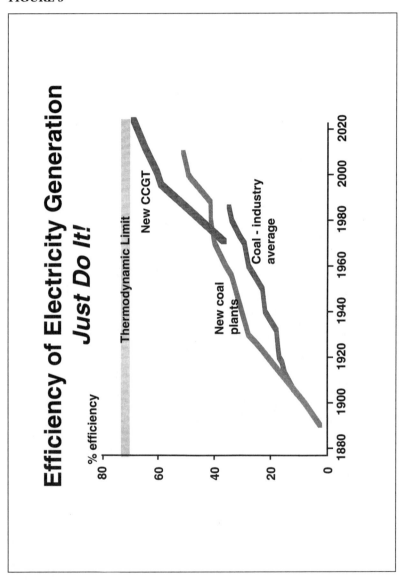

FIGURE 6

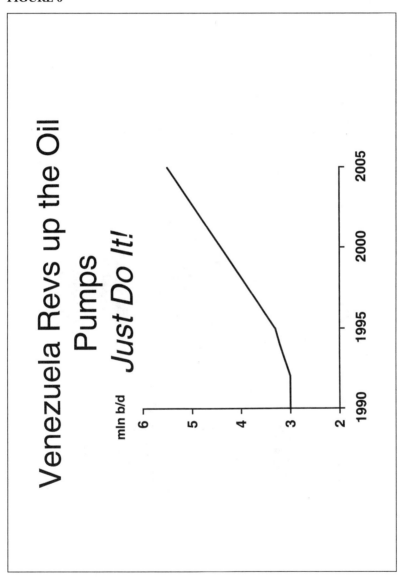

FIGURE 7

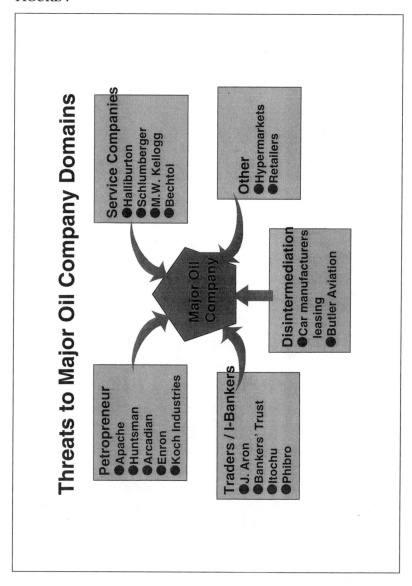

FIGURE 8

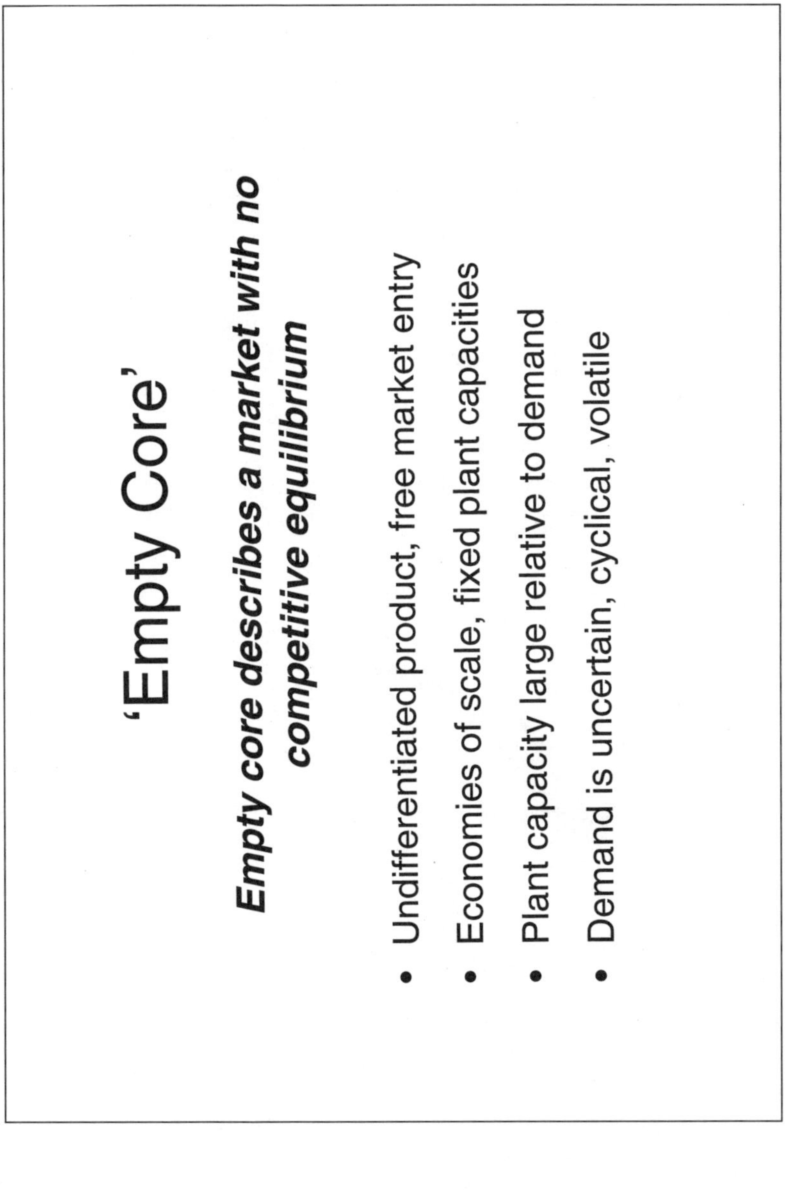

'Empty Core'

Empty core describes a market with no competitive equilibrium

- Undifferentiated product, free market entry
- Economies of scale, fixed plant capacities
- Plant capacity large relative to demand
- Demand is uncertain, cyclical, volatile

FIGURE 9

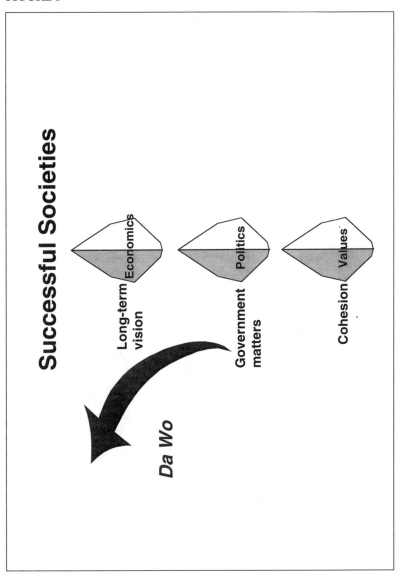

FIGURE 10

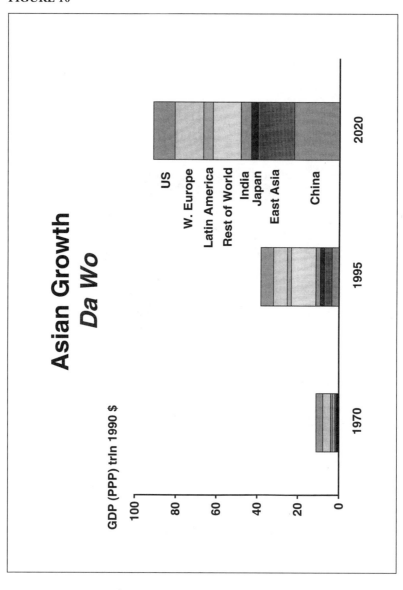

FIGURE 11

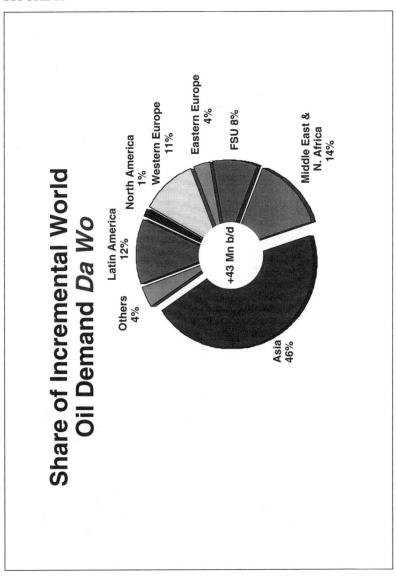

FIGURE 12

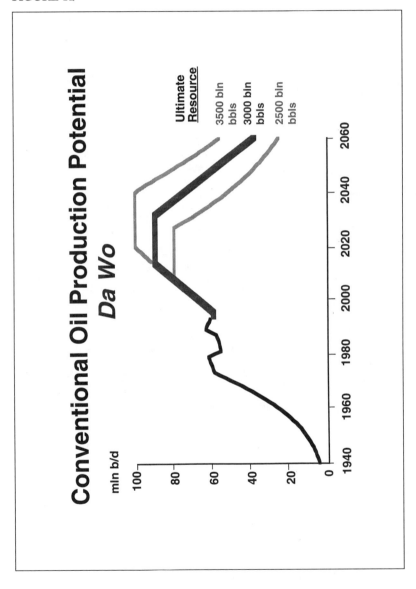

FIGURE 13

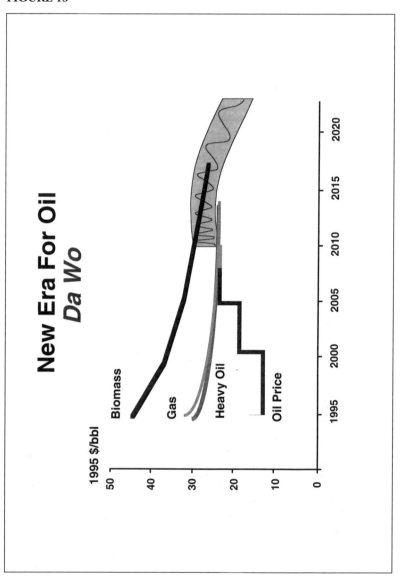

FIGURE 14

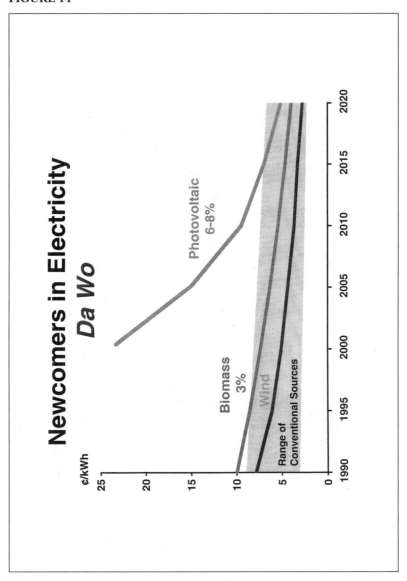

FIGURE 15

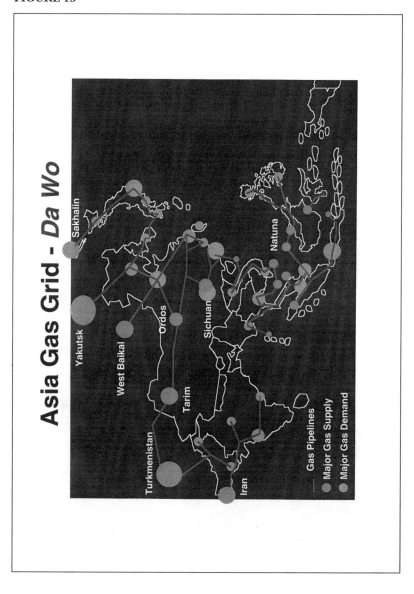

FIGURE 16

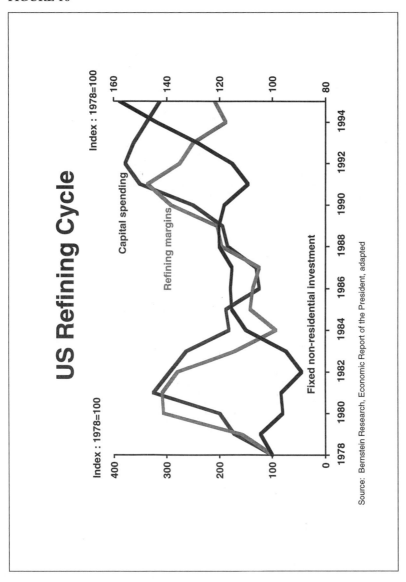

Source: Bernstein Research, Economic Report of the President, adapted

Appendix VI
Winning in Global Electric Power

Les Silverman
McKinsey & Company

FIGURE 1

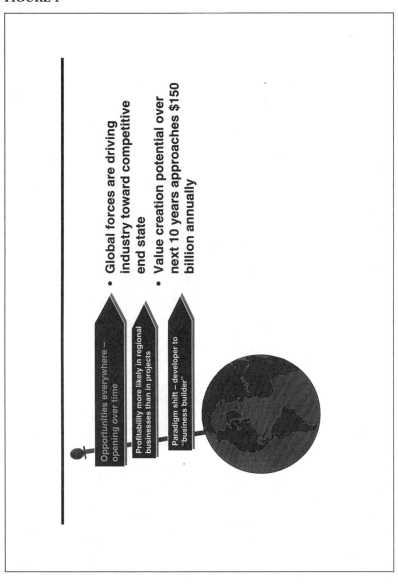

FIGURE 2

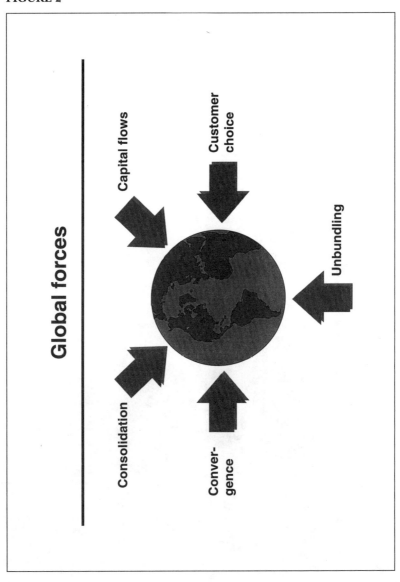

FIGURE 3

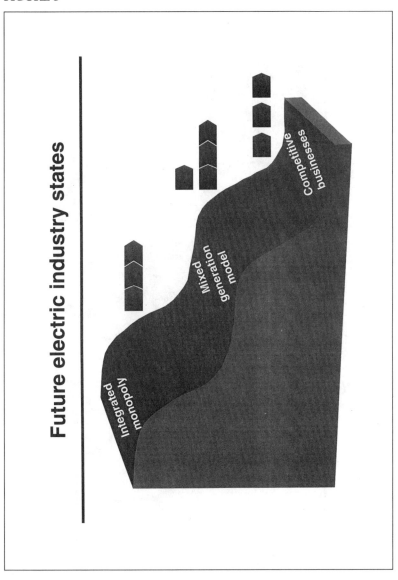

Future electric industry states

Integrated monopoly

Mixed generation model

Competitive businesses

FIGURE 4

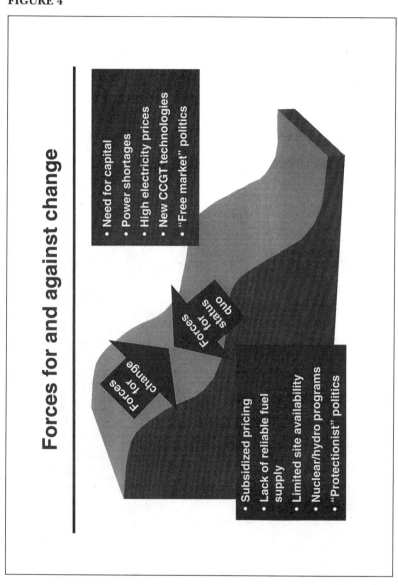

FIGURE 5

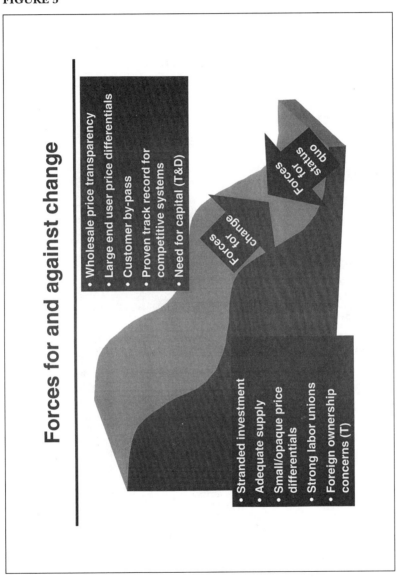

Forces for and against change

Forces for change

Forces for status quo

- Wholesale price transparency
- Large end user price differentials
- Customer by-pass
- Proven track record for competitive systems
- Need for capital (T&D)

- Stranded investment
- Adequate supply
- Small/opaque price differentials
- Strong labor unions
- Foreign ownership concerns (T)

FIGURE 6

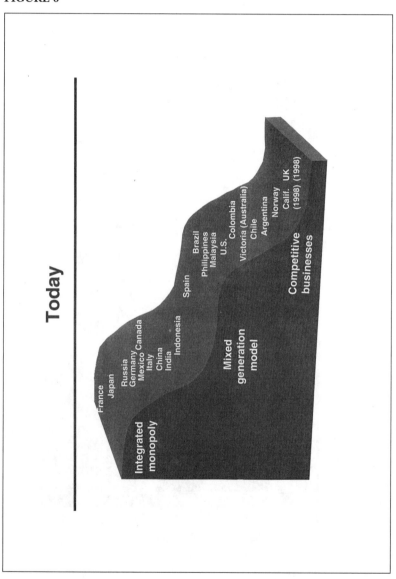

FIGURE 7

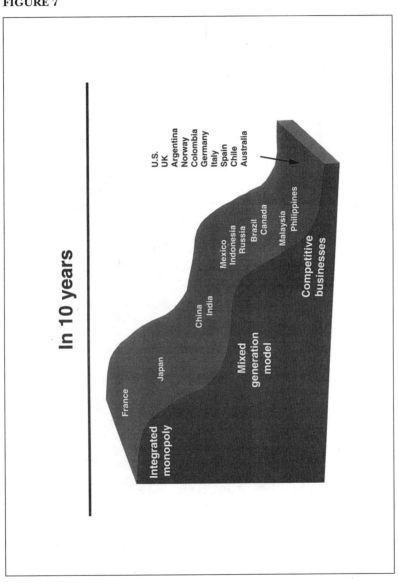

FIGURE 8

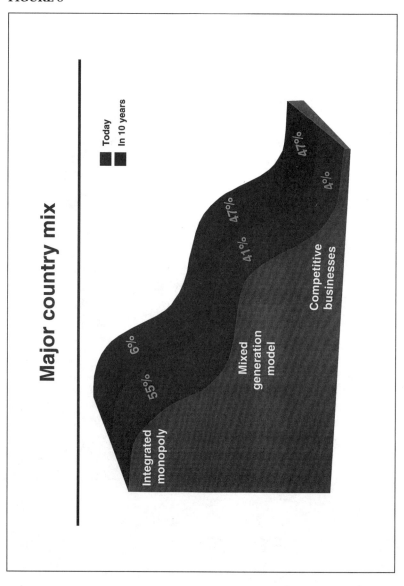

FIGURE 9

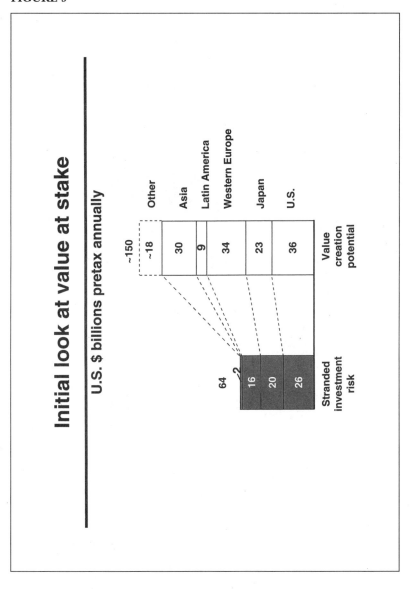

Initial look at value at stake

U.S. $ billions pretax annually

	Value creation potential	Stranded investment risk
	~150	64
Other	~18	~2
Asia	30	16
Latin America	9	
Western Europe	34	20
Japan	23	
U.S.	36	26

FIGURE 10

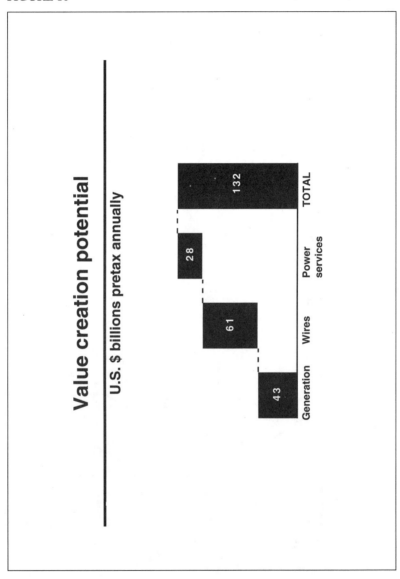

FIGURE 11

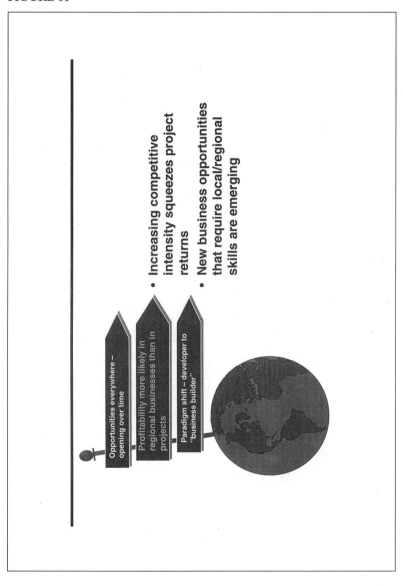

FIGURE 12

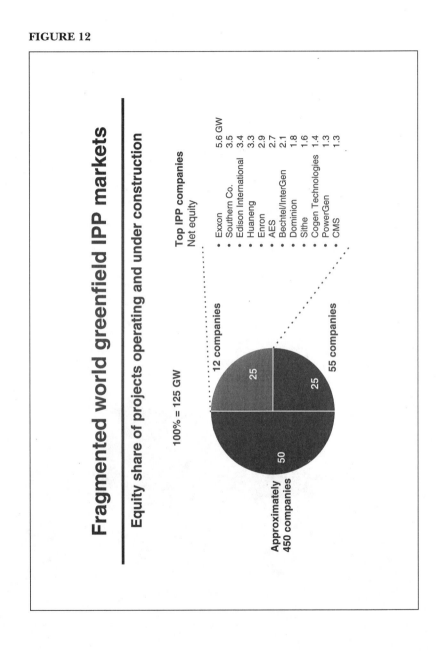

Fragmented world greenfield IPP markets

Equity share of projects operating and under construction

100% = 125 GW

Top IPP companies
Net equity

- Exxon   5.6 GW
- Southern Co.   3.5
- Edison International 3.4
- Huaneng   3.3
- Enron   2.9
- AES   2.7
- Bechtel/InterGen   2.1
- Dominion   1.8
- Sithe   1.6
- Cogen Technologies   1.4
- PowerGen   1.3
- CMS   1.3

12 companies

25

25

55 companies

50

Approximately
450 companies

FIGURE 13

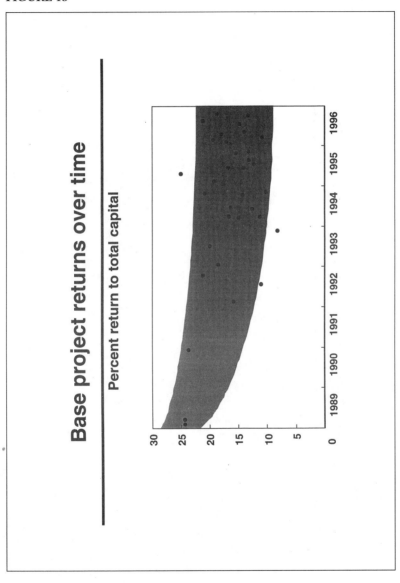

FIGURE 14

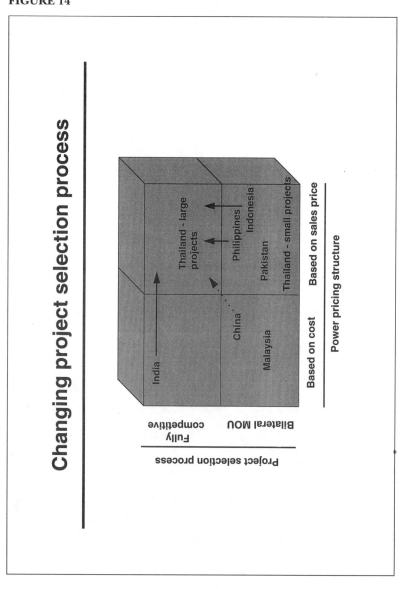

FIGURE 15

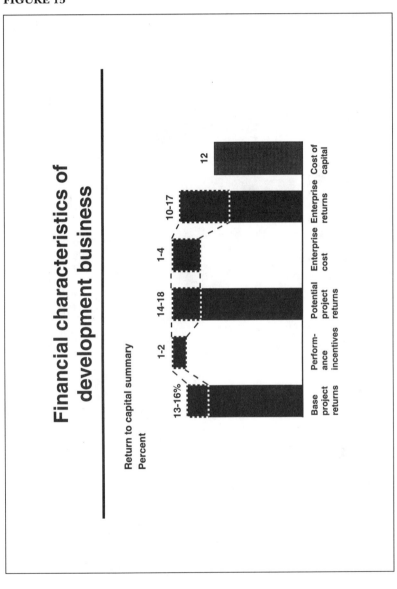

FIGURE 16

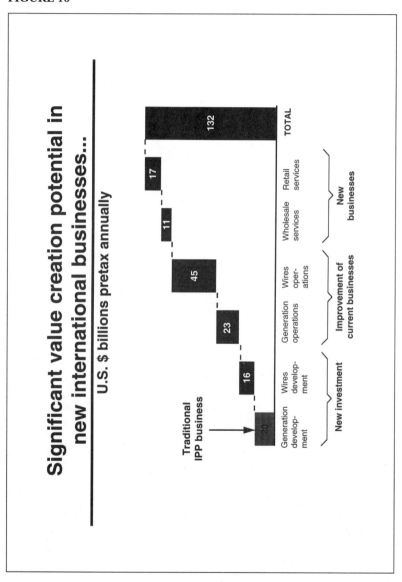

FIGURE 17

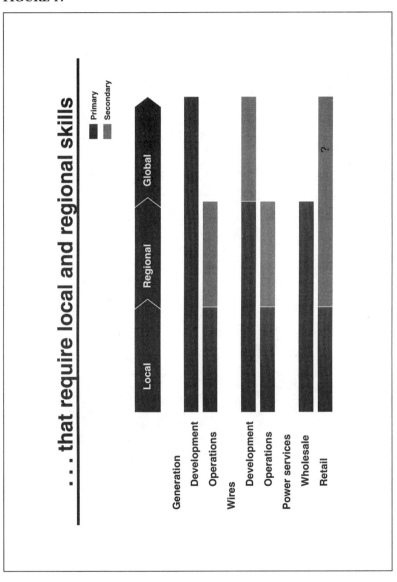

FIGURE 18

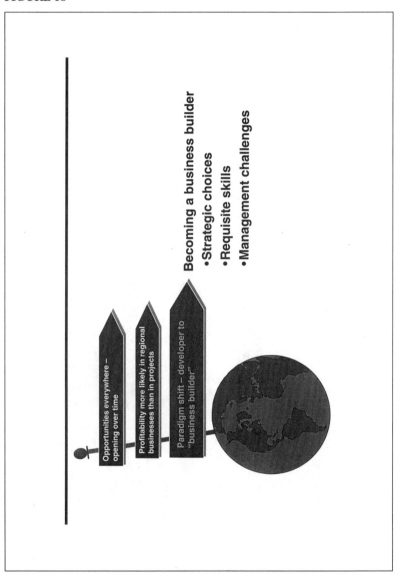

FIGURE 19

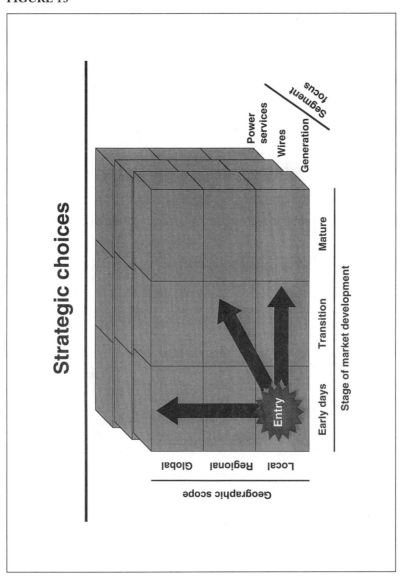

FIGURE 20

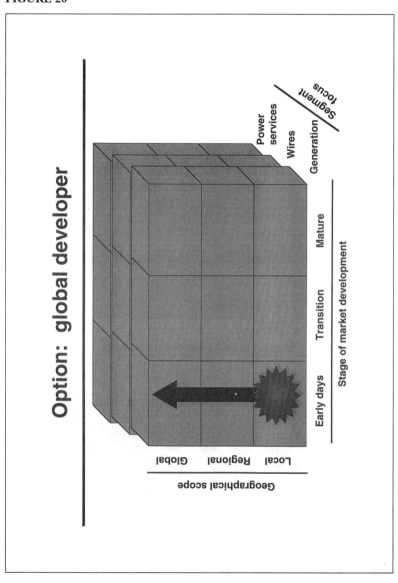

FIGURE 21

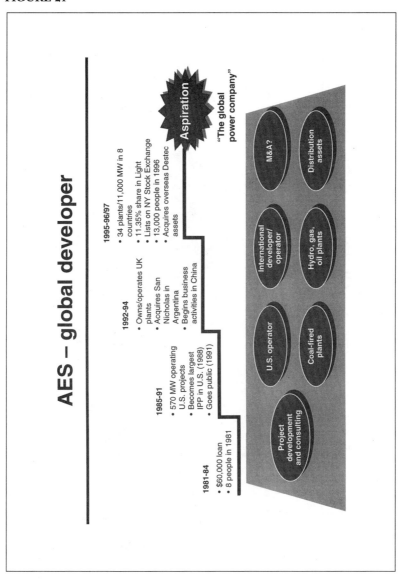

FIGURE 22

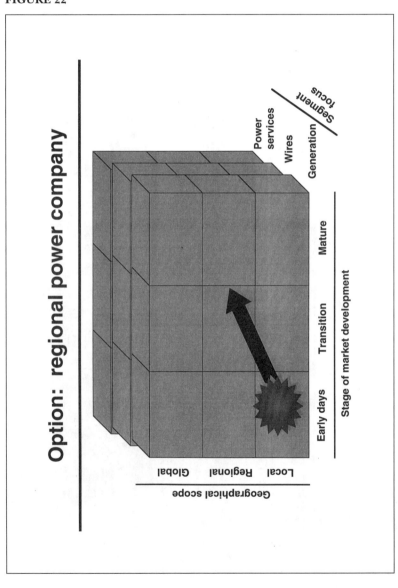

FIGURE 23

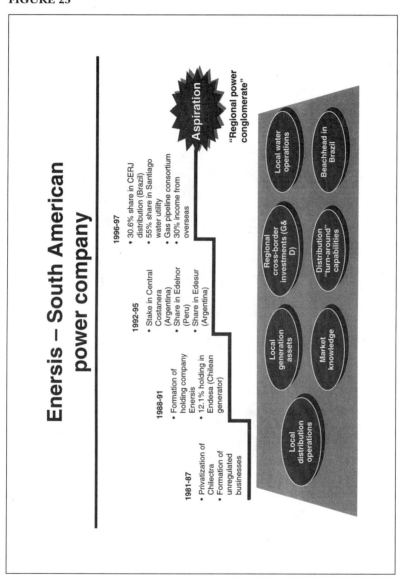

FIGURE 24

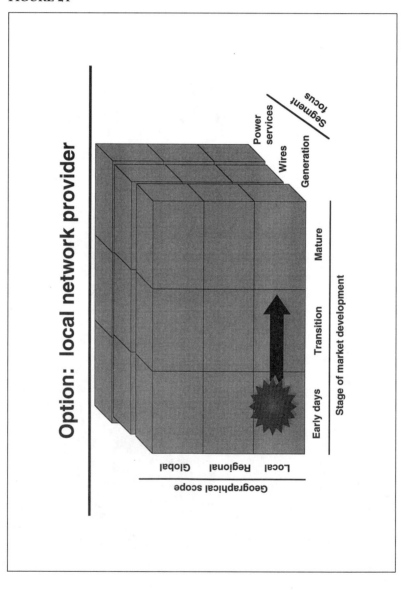

FIGURE 25

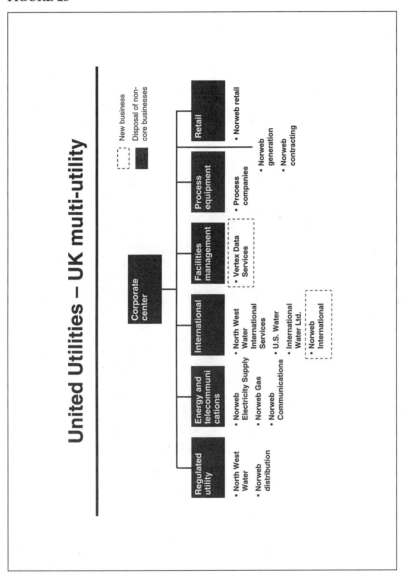

United Utilities – UK multi-utility

FIGURE 26

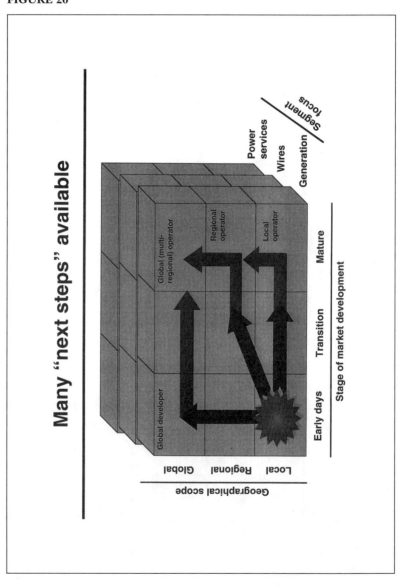

FIGURE 27

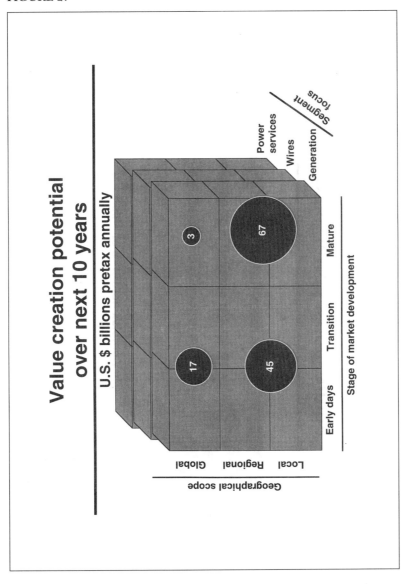